How to Deal With Difficult People

Effective Strategies to Deal with Difficult People

(How to Effectively Communicate and End Conflict with Difficult People)

Richard Horn

Published By **Kate Sanders**

Richard Horn

All Rights Reserved

Introverts: How Introverts Can Find Love and Have Better Relationships (Practical Tools to Leverage Your Strengths and Expand Your Network)

ISBN 978-1-7382986-1-7

No part of this guidebook shall be reproduced in any form without permission in writing from the publisher except in the case of brief quotations embodied in critical articles or reviews.

Legal & Disclaimer

The information contained in this book is not designed to replace or take the place of any form of medicine or professional medical advice. The information in this book has been provided for educational & entertainment purposes only.

The information contained in this book has been compiled from sources deemed reliable, and it is accurate to the best of the Author's knowledge; however, the Author cannot guarantee its accuracy and validity and cannot be held liable for any errors or omissions. Changes are periodically made to this book. You must consult your doctor or get professional medical advice before using any of the suggested remedies, techniques, or information in this book.

Upon using the information contained in this book, you agree to hold harmless the Author from and against any damages, costs, and expenses, including any legal fees potentially resulting from the application of any of the information provided by this guide. This disclaimer applies to any damages or injury caused by the use and application, whether directly or indirectly, of any advice or information presented, whether for breach of contract, tort, negligence, personal injury, criminal intent, or under any other cause of action.

You agree to accept all risks of using the information presented inside this book. You need to consult a professional medical practitioner in order to ensure you are both able and healthy enough to participate in this program.

Table Of Contents

Chapter 1: What Makes Them Difficult?...1

Chapter 2: Who's The Pain Within The Neck? 21

Chapter 3: How To Communicate 55

Chapter 4: Be Assertive 81

Chapter 5: What To Do When You're Attacked 98

Chapter 6: How To Deal With A Passive Aggressive 116

Chapter 7: The 10 Annoying Human Characteristics.. 125

Chapter 8: How To Grow Your Empathy For A Difficult Person 132

Chapter 9: Taking Control Of Your Own Difficult Behavior 139

Chapter 10: Dealing With Difficult People In Conflict 148

Chapter 11: Dealing With Difficult Coworkers 159

Chapter 12: Dealing With Difficult Boss At Workplace 172

Chapter 13: Dealing With Difficult Family Members 179

Chapter 1: What Makes Them Difficult?

Before moving into the manner to deal with hard humans, it is vital to outline what makes someone hard. Do you understand everybody for your existence that constantly makes you experience terrible, angry, pissed off, misunderstood, unheard, worn-out, and forced? That man or woman is difficult. These human beings can act in techniques that don't align with primary ethics. They haven't any trouble taking advantage of others. Some pass round sowing seeds of discord and mistrust truly because of the truth they sense locate it irresistible. They're those who are in no manner easy in communiqué because they might alternatively say a few aspect apart from what they in fact experience or count on.

Difficult humans don't apprehend what it manner to cooperate with others. They do their exquisite to get out of being held liable for their moves. You can't expect them to honor their commitments, both. They're the maximum terrible people within the room, and you could relaxation confident they'll poke holes in all your thoughts, irrespective of how right they are, without volunteering a better opportunity. The difficult person in your lifestyles might be a colleague, a "buddy," a decide, an in-law, or your boss at paintings. It may be the manager that maintains to call for an increasing number of of you, by no means satisfied even together with your brilliant paintings. It also can be the brother that makes a trouble of announcing subjects to damage your temper even as some element right occurs to you. There's additionally the patron disturbing to see the manager for some thing that shouldn't be a big deal.

When you discover your self in a hard state of affairs, it's herbal to surprise how you blundered your manner into it and what you could do to save you it from taking place within the destiny. You begin to marvel if what you're feeling and thinking is even correct. The exquisite man or woman has you thinking your intentions and sanity, and from time to time you find yourself appearing in techniques that you realize are out of character for you. In truth, you commonly understand and search for tactics to get collectively with others. The question then becomes, who's at fault right proper right here? You ask your self, "Am I the drama?" It doesn't assist that there are instances whilst it's now not smooth to inform if the opposite man or woman is actively searching out to frustrate you or in case you're the only who doesn't recognize the manner to have interaction with them.

It's one element to address a youngster going via puberty, however it's each specific handling a determine or friend who keeps to poke holes in all your choices and actions. You may also additionally have become so used to the frustration that you've decided to accept that this is the kind of person they're, or, on the turn factor, you can find they're sincerely intolerable and a drain in your pride. Something you endure in thoughts hard in a superb situation might not be tough in a totally particular instance. It additionally doesn't help that some difficult people are as slippery as eels. While some are very in advance approximately their disdain for you (making it smooth so that you can recognize what's taking area), others may be hard to pin down. You get the revel in that your interactions with them are off sufficient to make you revel in irritated. So on one give up of the spectrum, you've got the brazenly competitive, tough individual, and, on the possibility, you have were given the covert and passive one. Then there are folks that are smack dab within the middle of that spectrum; the passive-aggressive people. These can be very manipulative and are in no way sincere approximately a few component.

Overtly Aggressive, Difficult People

The exquisite factor about people who act aggressively is that it's hard to mistake their intentions for some aspect else. They're very open about the truth that they're antagonizing you. It can be very harsh talking with them, as they get opposed. Their display of pressure often intimidates others, as they have a tendency to yell and take in more place. Sometimes they get downright abusive. No count number what can also have precipitated them, large or small, you can anticipate they'll overreact.

Those who're competitive will do things like interrupting you at the equal time as you're talking or speaking over you. They don't have any hassle dismissing your tips, even when they're valid or terrific. They don't realise the which means of the phrase compromise and are typically a hair motive away from blowing their lids. They often experience it's miles their God-given proper to make their problem, whether or not it makes sense or no longer. For them, it's no longer "my manner or the motorway." It's "my way or no other way."

The aggressive, difficult character desires to manipulate the entirety and each person. They want the whole lot to align with how they see the arena and aren't willing to tolerate special viewpoints. The greater they awareness on their attitude, the greater tough it's far to get alongside facet them. They will overwhelm you into submission if you allow them to. They act this manner due to the fact it's far vital to make certain the whole thing takes vicinity steady with their plan and time table. They may be stimulated thru the reality that within the past, they've had their expectations now not play out as predicted. So, they select to be tough now due to the truth they'd alternatively manage topics to get the desired final results. If they get the concept that they're being criticized unfairly or someone's trying to get the better hand, they react with aggression. It only affords greater gas to the fireside after they experience like they're being cheated, overlooked, or misunderstood.

It's vital to don't forget that there's a difference amongst being irritated and being competitive. Anger is in fact an emotion. Just because of the truth you're irritated doesn't suggest you're going to behave aggressively. For instance, you will be having a heated debate with someone on a sensitive trouble and get mad, but you don't have to yell or ruin matters to show your anger. On the turn component, one can be aggressive whilst now not having that aggression fueled with the useful resource of anger. For example, a person may additionally offer you with grimy appears or name you names with out feeling indignant. Aggressive movement can play out in two techniques:

Impulsive

Instrumental

Impulsive aggression is a response to a few factor that occurs to someone. It comes, without a belief. It's from the sensation of being indignant. However, instrumental aggression isn't pushed through using anger but is a tool wielded to get a specific response out of you. For instance, if someone were to slap you for no in reality motive and you slap them decrease back, that is probably impulsive aggression in your component. However, count on a coworker criticizes you horribly at the same time as you're both in a meeting along facet your boss. In that case, the display of aggression right here is instrumental because the coworker is making an attempt to get your boss to apprehend that they're extra deserving of the promoting than you're.

Passive Aggressive Difficult People

Where competitive conduct is straightforward to look at, passive-competitive conduct is trickier. Passive-competitive humans are very oblique about what they want from their interactions with you, making them rather hard to cope with. They're very underhanded inside the manner they act. On the floor, it is able to seem like the entirety is exceptional and uneventful, however in their minds, there's a number of anger and resentment brewing, and this inadvertently comes out of their phrases and movements in subtle methods that may go away you feeling off.

The passive-aggressive character is opposed in the direction of you, but they cowl it in a way that has you feeling harassed about the situation. They'll in no way allow you to understand what they're thinking about you, and as a stop quit end result, you find yourself feeling annoyed and dissatisfied, but you surprise when you have any proper to experience the manner you do. Instead of telling you without delay what they'd like, they cover their hostility, inactively resisting each concept you recommend. For them to have manipulate of the situation, they want to control your thoughts and feelings with out seeming like that's what they're attempting to find to do.

When it comes to their terms, they're very ambiguous. Their lips say one detail, however their movements or tone of voice say a few issue else completely. For example, they will frequently turn to sarcasm, make jokes that don't sense like jokes to you simplest to comply with them up with "I become best kidding, loosen up," or can help you apprehend there's no longer some element wrong once they sense everything is wrong. If you could't shake the sensation that they're mendacity and you make a decision to name them out on it, they get dissatisfied with you. They desire muttering their displeasure, or they do things like slamming the door a touch too difficult and loudly. They may also roll their eyes or cuss you out beneath their breath.

The passive-competitive man or woman is a grasp at playing the victim. They're by no means at fault. For them, there's no such element as being accountable. You ought to in no way persuade them that they also had a detail to play in irrespective of the problem is, even when the evidence is staring them within the face. They'll act coldly within the direction of you and walk spherical with a pout to get your interest. They make you experience horrible for them, blaming anyone else for their problems although the blame is out of place. They may additionally moreover make you revel in liable for how they're feeling in that second and blissfully forget about the reality that they're the best reason they experience the way they do.

Since the passive-competitive character wears disguised hostility as armor, it's not constantly clean to inform after they're in action. Sometimes, it is able to seem they're in reality for your aspect and inclined to cooperate, however supply them time and the possibility, and that they'll do a little element to sabotage you and your plans. They may additionally additionally pick out out to live silent on the same time as their enter is sorely wished, handiest to show around and declare they knew your ideas wouldn't paintings at the identical time as you have been compelled to offer you with answers for the reason that they wouldn't offer their assist.

Other passive-competitive behaviors encompass:

Showing as much as meetings past due.

Delaying some aspect they said they'd help you with.

Procrastinating.

They're continuously complete of excuses for why they act the way they do, and those excuses may be right sufficient to offer them possible deniability. They also can moreover drum up nonexistent issues to frustrate you. They may additionally want to pick to be bad at their technique if meaning you're going to be frustrated or it's going to make you appearance awful.

One thing to check approximately passive-aggressive people is that some aren't aware of how manipulative they're — at the least, now not consciously. Their disguised hostility — on occasion even to themselves — makes it tough for every of you to resolve the problem that added approximately the passive-competitive conduct within the first area. The ones who are aware of what they're doing are certainly as difficult to deal with due to the truth they'd as an opportunity not communicate the real troubles amongst you.

People select to be passive-aggressive because of the truth they don't think it's their region to talk their minds for something motive. They don't suppose expressing their actual feelings and mind is right. This self-censorship is conduct they have a look at from stories in which they've been taught that their expressions are wrong and want to be stored to themselves. They get passive-aggressive due to the fact they're frightened of handling battle of words or being underneath a person's thumb.

There's additionally the component of not being confident enough to stick up for themselves. In the past, this tough person may additionally have tried to particular their mind most effective to get backlash. So they though pick out out to precise themselves in a good deal an awful lot much less apparent strategies due to the truth the passive-aggressive person is all subjects but not a doormat. They may want to as an opportunity assault you with a million microaggressions than roll over and passively receive your way of doing matters. They're no longer particular at asserting themselves.

Also, they're usually each the victim or the terrible man or woman within the room. As the sufferer, of their minds, humans are generally antagonizing them. It doesn't keep in mind whether or not or now not the antagonism is actual or imagined. They don't do well with disapproval and hate it whilst you don't take transport of as proper with them. They make you begin to censor yourself round them. They're additionally touchy to rejection, searching out signs and symptoms and symptoms that they're being excluded from subjects. Ironically, they're frequently proper approximately being excluded, however it's far frequently due to their victim thoughts-set. No one desires them with their horrible, woe-is-me mind-set there. They additionally love to behave as martyrs, telling you the manner a splendid deal time and power they've invested into subjects and those, most effective to get not anything again.

When the passive-aggressive character is the terrible one within the room, they commonly don't understand they're being tough to cope with. They get others worked up pretty with out trouble because of the truth they're those who can see the problems in every thought or how subjects should without problem turn out badly. They're exquisite at dampening the temper in the room because of the truth they're whole of mistrust and are regularly very pessimistic humans. They're satisfactory buddies with worry, regularly considering subjects others don't. They also typically tend to catastrophize minor troubles due to the fact the end of the arena.

With these people, it's difficult to appearance the first-class in something, and that terrible air of thriller they've got is powerful contagious. They are masters of discouragement and can make you prevent dreaming or in search of to move after your goals. If you permit them to get into your head, you may subsequently grow to be much like them or their notion of you.

Passive People

Passive human beings do not explicit what they're feeling or wondering. Sometimes, the passive man or woman is the human beings pleaser at paintings, who prefers to allow truely everybody have their manner and keeps to say certain to obligations they recognize they don't have sufficient time or energy to cope with. They'll do what anybody else is looking of them because they pull away on the idea of announcing no to others' wishes. Rather than make it smooth that they have got their options, they live silent for fear of being controversial or ruffling feathers. They received't say a issue till someone else speaks up, after which they'll go with the entirety the alternative man or woman says. This form of individual may be as an opportunity clingy, too.

People pleasers work hard to assuage others. They fawn over others in the want of getting them on their side. However, the hassle with this approach is that it rubs absolutely everyone the wrong manner. It's no longer fantastic at the identical time as they say positive to the entirety best to will will let you down due to the reality they don't understand their limits. As a stop end end result, human beings pleasers wind up ruining relationships. Their passive behavior performs out as doing the entirety others need. Another way you can check their passivity is in their desire now not to take part in some thing, just so they don't want to take obligation for the outcomes. At first, they appear very clean to narrate with, however in due time, it's smooth to look that they don't convey some issue to the table. They decide upon others to step in and get matters finished in place of initiate matters. They not often make picks, which may be traumatic for whoever they're with.

Chapter 2: Who's The Pain Within The Neck?

Now which you've seen how hard people suppose and act, it's time to take an extended, hard examine your self to appearance the manner you usually respond to others. To kick off this financial disaster, proper proper right here's a list of statements you need to test. If any of them applies to you, write a YES beside it.

If someone ruins my plans, I start contemplating strategies I can real my revenge.

When I cope with someone tough, I depart the interaction thinking about who've been the winners and losers in that spherical.

If someone makes me experience horrible, I usually tend to revel in volatile and open to further attacks.

I usually revel in helpless at the same time as a conversation with someone doesn't bypass how I wanted it to.

Sometimes, I get jealous of others who preserve to head after their desires or the consequences they want.

When I virtually have a heated argument with someone, it looks as if they one manner or the alternative find out a way to make the whole thing my fault.

I continuously concede to unique people's dreams, even if I don't experience love it.

Nothing irritates me more than at the same time as others get away with awful conduct.

It appears like people maintain planning and leaving me out of them.

I get quite dissatisfied whilst others are acting difficult, because it appears they're looking to make me mad.

I can't shake the feeling that many humans don't understand me.

When someone has an opinion towards mine, I have a propensity to assume of things in phrases of who's proper or incorrect.

Whenever a person criticizes me, I get the enjoy that I've been attacked.

I usually generally tend to do what all people else desires, although I don't want to.

It's hard to forget conversations with tough people, as I will be predisposed to ruminate over who said what.

Did you answer certain to numerous the ones statements? Then the opportunities are which you will be predisposed to consider your worldwide in terms of you in desire to others. In different phrases, you normally will be predisposed to absolve your self of all duty for problem on your interactions. The manner you notice it, the problems that rise up are not your fault, or there may be now not whatever that you could have finished to make the scenario better.

Interestingly, your default assumption even as it looks as if someone is being hard in their interactions with you is that they will be out to get you. You can't shake the sensation that they're intentionally searching out to oppose or lure you. You wish you may do something positive about the scenario but enjoy powerless. The most effective motive you experience powerless is that you don't have any idea what you may do to reply to the hassle constructively. Also, due to the fact you despise the sensation of being helpless, you'll an awful lot as an alternative blame a person else for the whole lot that's now not going proper.

Let's examine an example. David is 32 years antique. Since he have become a kid, his older brother, Jacob, had constantly been unserious approximately basketball. Their dad and mom habitually gave in to some thing Jacob desired. Leroy, their dad, might have been an incredible basketball player, as he loves to tell anybody. As Leroy moreover loves to inform each person, he sacrificed his basketball profession to stay at home and cope with his spouse and youngsters.

Ever considering he became a kid, David did his extraordinary to keep his mother and father satisfied with him. So up until now, he makes wonderful to name his dad and mom every day and go to them as a minimum two times a month. On the opportunity hand, Jacob couldn't tell us approximately his beyond. He nice indicates up whenever he feels find out it not possible to withstand. Their dad and mom throw pretty a few coins at Jacob and attend maximum of his video games. Whenever Jacob doesn't get his way, he gets truly indignant. In David's opinion, Jacob is as a substitute needy and honestly self-absorbed. So David well-knownshows it hard to be appropriate to Jacob every time they meet.

The response you pick while interacting with someone tough comes down to 3 elements.

The first factor you must bear in mind is who you're managing. Is this a person you are very familiar with? Is this individual usually a tough character to address? Are they in a position of authority over you? Are they someone dominant, like a discern, a bossy friend, or your supervisor?

The next detail to consider is the cause they're being tough. Is this person supplying you with a tough time because of the truth they're looking for to embarrass or undermine your art work? Could it certainly be that they're having a horrible day? Is this individual commonly hard to deal with for definitely everybody else?

The 1/3 detail is after they tend to be difficult. Were you already feeling terrible or inclined earlier than interacting with this man or woman? Has your day been specially tough?

The fourth detail is what's making them tough. Is the hassle you're each arguing approximately some thing you idea had already been taken care of out? Is the priority of the struggle of phrases some element fundamental or unimportant?

Next, you want to consider in which they may be choosing to be difficult. Is this man or woman performing the way they may be with others so that you can embarrass you? Or do they most effective act the manner they do with you while you're on my own, so no person can see them acting on this way?

The very last component to keep in mind is the way you sense. Are you careworn or tired? Do you revel in very uncomfortable and uncertain approximately dealing with this person again? Do you discover your self feeling harassed about what your rights are?

One detail stays the same, no matter who the difficult individual is, what it is that has them appearing in the manner they do, what their motivations are, in which they act in that way, or after they select out to act in that manner. They'll be tough to cope with if you observe that they're being difficult. One difficulty you could do is absolutely be for the reason that this is how they may usually behave. The detail you can do is select to attack them head-on, every at once or the use of passive-aggressive techniques. Either preference has upsides and drawbacks.

Choosing Acceptance

If a person does some issue terrible towards you or says horrible phrases, you can be given that this is how they are, and you may decide to do away with yourself from their presence. Instead of permitting them to understand what you're questioning and feeling or what you preference, you could select to live quiet due to the truth you aren't keen on warfare of phrases. You may additionally moreover furthermore determine that in place of fight them due to the fact you don't take delivery of as actual with them, you'd as an opportunity go with some thing they're doing or announcing. The odds of you talking up for yourself, reputation up for what's right, or going in the direction of what's incorrect are very low.

The query is, what should make you pick this reaction? Like David, your assumption might be that your speakme up could motive others to feel angry, harm, or disillusioned in you. The problem with accepting hard human beings and their behaviors is that it could reason them taking advantage of you constantly and disrespecting you. There are, but, some upsides to upcoming them on this manner.

Acceptance is a beneficial tool whilst the connection is essential, and also you cannot control to pay for to damage it via confronting them.

Accepting their conduct is a splendid manner to hold you from being harm bodily via the alternative character.

When the trouble being mentioned is more crucial to the other character than it is to you, it can be useful to truly accept their behavior.

If you're in a state of affairs in which you can not find out the cash for to have an escalation of the trouble to be had, it may be higher to simply accept what's taking region.

When it's a scenario wherein the possibility man or woman need to do what they need and discover on their very very own that they have got been incorrect, then accepting what's taking vicinity is the extraordinary path of motion.

Sometimes, you'll be wrong. In this situation, the practical preference is to simply accept what's occurring.

Indirect Hostile Confrontation

The trying to find engine doesn't be sincerely proper for you, and your revel in green with envy and unhappy approximately how the possibility man or woman is performing. You can also moreover choose out to reply in passive-aggressive strategies. But you may choose out to behave on this way because of the truth you're doing all your extremely good not to be confrontational, however you cannot assist your self. For instance, you may decide to use sarcastic remarks, complain masses approximately how the other person is behaving to others however in no manner to them, and so on. If you pick out out to reply on this way, you're fearful of expressing your resentment because of the reality you sense it's no longer secure to acquire this. You get the feeling that when you have been to explicit your evaluations and wishes right now, human beings might consider you as as an alternative selfish. Another issue you may be scared of is seeming impolite to others. You might also additionally now not have the self assurance to address the results of expressing your thoughts.

Instead of addressing the hassle at once, you select out to be passive-competitive. In your thoughts, as a minimum, you get to specific the reality that you are green with envy of the scenario or the man or woman. While this avoidant method may additionally furthermore relieve you, it's miles inefficient due to the truth the alternative human beings concerned within the situation haven't any concept what you be given as authentic with you studied or experience or what you want. However, from time to time, being oblique for your battle of phrases can be a bonus. Use this technique of warfare of phrases while you need to:

Stop the scenario from getting even worse than it already is.

Not have to cope with an actual war of words.

Make certain your hobbies stay blanketed.

Keep yourself or a person else stable.

Buy yourself some more time.

Direct Hostile Confrontation

When you pick out to be direct and confrontational, that means using pressure. You may additionally discover your self shouting and swearing on the man or woman or perhaps bodily attacking them. You choose out this reaction now not due to the fact you're usually a lousy person however due to the fact you've been misunderstood within the past. You're bored with feeling mistreated, disregarded, and undermined at every turn. You may also additionally have struggled with humiliation from similar conditions inside the beyond.

More regularly than not, the attitudes and actions of tough humans can be what ultimately deliver you off the threshold after several events that have persisted to live needlessly traumatic. You ultimately find out that you could no longer condone their behavior, so that you snap. Being competitive and confronting your opponent might be terrible because of the fact the already terrible scenario have to get worse. However, this is an super preference inside the following conditions:

When it's a scenario, whilst you want to manipulate it right away.

When you ought to show yourself greater effective than the alternative character.

When it's far important an high-quality way to do better than the other man or woman.

When you want to appearance results right now.

When you want to shield yourself or take some other motion speedy.

Assigning Blame to Others

There are upsides and disadvantages to being confrontational, whether or not overtly or covertly. More often than no longer, you can select to justify your actions in location of being chargeable for the way you reply on the identical time as you can't cope with a person's nasty behavior. You may additionally need to pick out to defend your self and blame the opportunity character for the motive you acted inside the manner you probable did. Whenever you've had a difficult face-off with a person that has left you feeling terrible, you may consequences assume that the other character is in reality chargeable for your emotions. This angle is how David selected to method subjects collectively together with his circle of relatives. He assumed that they've been the cause he's harboring resentment.

The trouble with blaming someone else is that it makes it difficult so that you can make any constructive changes to the scenario available. The cause is that in case you absolutely undergo in thoughts they'll be to be blamed and they spurred you on to behave as you possibly did, you're now not going to do some thing approximately finding an answer. Why should you, in any case, while it wasn't your fault? You're left in a willing function wherein there's now not whatever you may do approximately it. Blaming the possibility individual means that there's not anything you may or must do to alternate yourself or your responses. This assumption is an faulty one due to the fact no person has manipulate over the way you act. Holding this assumption will make it so you will in no way have the exquisite solutions in your issues, even if you suppose your line of concept is accurate.

Are You the Drama?

While it can now not enjoy find it irresistible in the warm temperature of the right now, no character's making you enjoy the way you enjoy. You're the best one chargeable for that. To recognize the way to consider the three components of emotion. First, there's the bodily element, which includes all your frame's responses even as you revel in a best way. Fear must cause you having a rapid heartbeat and shallow breathing. Then there's the behavioral component, which includes the actions you are taking because of fear. For instance, you could combat back or retreat for protection at the same time as anxious. Finally, there's the cognitive hassle, which comes all of the way all the way down to your beliefs. The cognitive a part of emotions is your mind and expectancies in the situation. For example, if you're afraid, you can anticipate, "If I don't get out of proper right here, some thing terrible will take place to me."

These three factors of feelings have an effect on each other. Your mind, ideals, and expectations regarding someone or scenario are what you experience such as you do. For instance, expect you're approximately to transport paragliding and need to jump from a top into the air. The manner you located and the thoughts you have were given are going to have an effect on the way you revel in approximately leaping off the edge. If that is a few factor you've constantly favored to do and are captivated with, you'd feel excited. However, if you're most effective doing this because of the truth someone made you, or it have become a dare or something, the probabilities are that what you believe you studied, consider, and assume could likely glaringly purpose you to revel in worried.

Just as paragliding can initiate you to assume and sense a certain manner, so can others initiate you to assume and feel subjects. However, provocation doesn't same causation. Paragliding doesn't reason worry or pleasure. In the same manner, people don't cause you to sense awesome or awful. The hassle isn't what someone else does however the way you choose out out to interpret it. Say you're awaiting a person to expose up for a meeting, and you get the feel that they're not worried that they've saved you ready. You may additionally moreover moreover experience upset through this. However, you may reflect onconsideration on this in another way. You need to understand that their being overdue has given you greater time to prepare and get in the suitable headspace for the assembly. In this situation, you wouldn't experience dissatisfied. You'd be grateful.

Do you seize yourself while you're approximately to shift blame onto distinct humans around you? Being liable for responding to troublesome people will make it a good buy easier as a manner to address them. The cause is that maintaining yourself accountable for your actions technique proudly owning them, which means that you have got extra energy over them. You can choose out actions more likely to get you the desired outcomes.

Learned Helplessness

Learned helplessness is a precept that states that if one or greater of your interactions with someone have commonly brought about unwanted results within the beyond, the percentages are you're going to discover ways to be helpless on every occasion you've got were given interplay with that individual. So you count on which you don't have any manage or have an effect on over them due to the truth they're unmanageable to you. At least, that's what you start to inform yourself approximately your interactions and their consequences. Fortunately, determined out helplessness may be unlearned. You must become aware of your vintage beliefs and choose greater empowering tremendous ones. The first step is to recognise why you and others pick certain moves. It's moreover particular to enter each interplay watching for some thing accurate.

We all have fantastic expectations approximately how we must and shouldn't be handled, and while others don't act in ways that align with the ones expectations, it's smooth to experience resentment and anger. For instance, David might also moreover choose Jacob to prevent depending so much on their mother and father and examine to take care of them as an opportunity. You ought to assume that the pals you've got must be dependable and type, or usually a pride to be with. You should in all likelihood count on that your coworkers should usually want to cooperate with you. So really, it's provoking at the identical time as those expectations aren't met. If you're taking it to coronary heart, you may turn out to be proper now or no longer right now confrontational, resigned, and passive. However, in case you express your harm, you'll probable grow to be competitive. Another alternative we haven't addressed is being direct and assertive whilst preserving a cool head. We will communicate that later.

Always bear in mind that the better your expectations are, the less complicated it's miles to be upset. However, the lower your expectancies are, the much more likely you will be used and taken advantage of. Expectations are often unconscious and extra a characteristic of addiction, this is why we get into war and misunderstand the human beings round us. No rule says a person need to behave the manner you anticipate them to, notwithstanding the fact that that is probably plenty better for you. It is crucial, therefore, so that you can determine out your expectations of others. You can acquire this with the aid of searching at what your very personal values are. Your values can also need to consist of honesty, punctuality, loyalty, electricity of will, kindness, gratitude, and so on. So make an effort to discern out what subjects to you the most, and you could proper away see what you expect from others.

You have to do your splendid to consider that no longer absolutely everyone has the equal values as you do. People aren't mechanically awful truly because their values range from yours, so that you don't need to come to be judgmental. You want to be extra flexible to your expectations and preserve them sensible. For instance, while maximum human beings could assume the way Jacob interacts together along together with his parents isn't great, it's first-class to realize that this conduct has end up set over a long time, and nothing David or each person else need to do will change that. So David need to end up more realistic in his expectancies of Jacob so we can have interaction higher. If you keep in mind without a doubt all people has to act in line with your expectations, you're normally going to find out your self interpreting the conditions you face in a horrible slight. You'll additionally be passing at the headache of your expectations to the opposite character, which in flip way you'll be tough to cope with yourself.

Learned helplessness has a domino effect in your relationships. It prevents you from looking to decorate your relationships. After you conquer located out helplessness, you'll be inspired. Then you'll find out it much less complex to enhance your relationships on your life. Here are three steps to triumph over located helplessness in your relationships:

Step 1: Change your wondering. Changing the manner you believe you studied is the maximum vital step to overcoming discovered out helplessness. Negative thoughts reason horrible behaviors and attitudes. Think of factors you cannot manage as a challenge in place of a setback. Challenge yourself not to give up.

Step 2: Gain optimism for the destiny (change your behavior). Challenge yourself to be positive about the future, even if you've been pessimistic inside the past. Try to provide your self a reason to be constructive. You'd be surprised at how lifestyles can trade on your want whilst you start to capture the day.

Step 3: Exercise and exercising interactive verbal exchange (enhance your relationships). Decide on belongings you need on your relationships that would help decorate them. Then, exercise the ones matters in interactive conditions with human beings you're close to. The extra you exercise active, nice interactions with others, the less difficult it's going to probably be that permits you to continuously engage undoubtedly with all of us round you. After you've triumph over determined out helplessness, you'll boom in self-efficacy, due to this you'll don't forget in your self and your ability to exchange subjects for your lifestyles. You can get keep of traumatic conditions without fear of failure. With improved self-efficacy, you'll be able to change the way you technique things in your lifestyles that aren't going for walks for you and encourage yourself to do the right issue in place of giving up even as some thing receives hard.

Positive Expectations

The way to be sensible to your expectancies from others is to be open in speaking just so no man or woman has to wager what you count on. These expectations range from immoderate expectations, notably lowering the kind of results you could get out of your interactions. Positive expectancies permit for a far wider form of answers and located you in a function where you're seeking out areas wherein you and the alternative person agree. Having terrific expectancies as opposed to excessive expectations is how you could avoid feeling taken gain of, indignant, or harm due to the fact you're now not preserving straight away to a inflexible set of expectancies you need the other person to satisfy. In David's case, he should take transport of that his dad and mom experience letting Jacob have his manner and don't experience green with envy in the course of him. This attention ought to indicate that David need to save you looking forward to too much of Jacob.

When you're engaged in a communique with someone difficult, it's smooth to attract the same antique conclusions approximately how they're always difficult to cope with. However, you shouldn't write them off. Instead, don't forget them as modern-day-day to you, this means that that you don't preserve on to your expectations of them. This way, you'll open your self as lots as higher interactions with them. For example, you can consider you're actually assembly them for the first time and don't recognize some aspect approximately them. When you accept as authentic with you studied of them as a person new, you permit yourself to answer to them in new techniques which might be higher for every of you. As you try this, don't be surprised if the opposite person receives protecting, suspicious, or indignant with you. You need to think via the viable effects of your alternatives earlier than you do something special, and at the same time as you exchange subjects, be regular. You want to moreover be flexible in trying to find answers but never provide in.

Know Your Rights

Everyone has their rights below the law. You moreover have private rights, which may be your perceptions about the way you ought to be dealt with. Sticking up in your rights stops others from maltreating you. Your rights are rooted in your values, because of this if you value honesty, as an instance, you recollect you have got were given the right to expect the fact at all times. It is vital to check in with yourself to make certain that you enlarge the ones rights to all and sundry else you engage with. Here are some rights you can resonate with:

The right to talk and think as you revel in.

The right to ask for what you want.

The right to select out.

The right to decide.

The right to exchange your mind.

The right to be in the wrong.

The right to achieve success.

The proper to upward push up for what you endure in mind in.

The proper to parent out what matters to you.

The right to no longer understand or no longer recognize a few element.

The right to request more data or statistics.

The right to privacy.

The proper to independence.

The proper to take away yourself from a scenario.

The right to now not help.

The proper to now not be held chargeable for someone else's movements, feelings, or troubles.

The proper to be glad.

The right to expect the truth from human beings.

If you could think about precise rights to encompass within the listing above, you need to do so. Remember, values and rights are subjective. Just as you've got got a right to stick up to your rights, others have the proper to brush aside them. However, understanding your rights will help you place smooth boundaries so that you're no longer exploited. To do this, you want to be confident approximately letting others recognize what's and isn't okay.

Confidence Is Key

You can't permit others recognize your goals, goals, and boundaries without self notion. Confidence is all approximately what you don't forget you're able to. So if you need to deal with difficult humans effects, you need to trust it's viable for you. You can become this kind of people who've no problem interacting with hard characters, are unafraid of confrontation, and are prepared to deal with consequences. When you're confident that you may deal with all people to your life constructively, you don't want to control other people's mind or feelings, and you're open to whatever they want to speak. Being assured doesn't advocate you'll in no manner experience disturbing, but the factor is that you don't allow the tension save you you from expressing your self. So, expertise your rights and values and having brilliant expectations allows you have greater self belief in handling these humans. Confidence and courage aren't much like in no way being afraid. Rather, those things are about acting as in case you're now not afraid, regardless of the fact that you may be.

Chapter 3: How To Communicate

Now which you've considered how your responses to others, what you count on, and what you believe about how they want to act have an impact in your interactions, it's time to reflect onconsideration on the manner to talk better. It's not the very best hassle to understand what to mention when topics get heated, but communique is extra than sincerely speaking. It's a lower again-and-forth affair, which means you ought to talk and pay hobby efficiently. You'll apprehend what to mention at the same time as you apprehend the way to pay attention.

Usually, while human beings have interaction with others, they're in no way listening. They bypass beforehand to make assumptions that may or won't be accurate, in particular at the same time as addressing hard problems. Their mind-set can distort the message being communicated, each on the element of the listener or the speaker. Sometimes you may think what they're going to say, in any other case you get the texture which you received't have the ability to mention your piece, so you jump in with interruptions that further complicate things.

Sometimes it's a rely number of being forced about what the opposite character is announcing, this means that you're processing their terms with a chunk of a lag at the back of what they're presently announcing. You're additionally tempted to song out the alternative individual, particularly while you enjoy like they're complaining, whining, or being too aggressive. You'll understand that tuning them out doesn't prevent them because of the reality they may see you're not listening, and they'll hold at it.

Being an Active Listener

Fortunately, you can test a piece a few factor referred to as lively listening. There are vital advantages to lively listening. For one element, there can be no way you can mistake what the opportunity person is making an attempt to tell you, and, for every extraordinary, it's an awful lot less complicated as a way to interact with them well because you recognize them higher. If you preserve experiencing verbal exchange gaps, lively listening will help you. This machine includes being proactive and listening to the opportunity person, proceeding to apprehend what they're pronouncing and what's motivating them to say it. When you do that, you'll be able to get this right. Active listening is an powerful way to manner information and have to be used within the route of conversations for the speaker to get keep of the entire charge of the phrases being spoken. The speaker feels understood, desired, and confirmed.

Active listening is prepared referring to someone to make them feel better. It's about knowledge and empathizing with a person, commiserating with them on the equal time as they're disenchanted or can't recognize what you suggest. How heaps do you invest in your relationships? Do you are taking study of the way you have got interaction with human beings? If so, then energetic listening can be a awesome functionality to expand. Active listening additionally encourages distinct humans to speak approximately themselves extra in my opinion. You're much more likely to offer the right shape of comments within the event that they start speaking. Or they will even percentage some element that would help you beautify your process abilities. In brief, energetic listening allows you come to be a better communicator, that may be a key a part of constructing particular relationships at art work. It's moreover surely accurate on your career.

Using Minimal Encouragers

You can use nonverbal conversation to signify to the opposite character that you're paying attention to them. For instance, you could shake your head even as you don't agree with what they're pronouncing or nod if you agree. You can also ensure which you set up eye contact with them. All of those are known as minimal encouragers. Using phrases like "fine," "oh," and "uh huh" can assist the alternative individual understand that you are listening to them. Use them enough instances that they recognize you're listening, but not masses that they start to experience including you're interrupting them. When discussing with a difficult character, use those minimal encouragers in a neutral tone. Don't be sarcastic or angry.

Using Reflective Listening

This unique talent makes it easy to the person you're talking with how masses you've understood them. To practice this, you're going to should reputation. Reflective listening requires 3 elements:

Repeating

Summarizing

Paraphrasing

Repeating is virtually the system of announcing what the alternative character has told you. You try this due to the fact you want to ensure which you've heard them efficaciously. Repeating what they've stated does now not robotically mean which you undergo in thoughts them. It's definitely you confirming that you've understood them efficiently.

Summarizing is the manner of summing up the whole lot they've knowledgeable you. It's basically approximately taking the principle factors that they've made and summarizing them. Summarizing is a way that guarantees you could live on subject matter when discussing a scenario in choice to fending off on tangents. Finally, there's the detail of paraphrasing. When you paraphrase what the alternative individual has said, you're saying what they stated, however in a particular manner. A right rule of thumb is first of all the resource of way of announcing:

"Let's see if I actually have this immediately up to now…"

"Am I proper in assuming you suggest…"

"Are you trying to inform me…"

"I count on you're saying…"

When summarizing and paraphrasing, you're the use of your terms to unique what you've understood from what the opportunity person has said. When you've finished summarizing or paraphrasing, you need to wrap it up via manner of asking them, "Do I actually have that right?" or a few factor to that impact. Asking those questions is crucial because it will permit them to affirm which you have certainly understood what they're saying properly. They can with out problems make clear or correct you even as the other is the case, saving you unnecessary arguments.

Sometimes it's a amazing concept to overstate or understate a few factor that you are paraphrasing or summarizing. For example, count on someone believes which you haven't been information or listening. In that case, you may make clear thru the use of asking, "So do you observed I continually lessen you off even as you communicate, and I in no manner pay attention?" They also can moreover then be compelled to make clean that they don't enjoy that manner approximately you all the time.

If you haven't idea approximately it already, continuously summarizing or paraphrasing what the opportunity character says all the time will appear a bit ordinary. The critical thing approximately the ones communication elements is which you must listen as in case you had been going to summarize or paraphrase. You don't constantly ought to do so. The critical trouble about reflective listening is getting you to channel your interest to the message being conveyed to you so that you don't feel tempted to break. Reflecting makes the alternative man or woman experience which consist of you've heard them, clearly so they don't want to copy their factors or assault you. When coping with tough human beings, the warfare is analyzing to stay calm even if the state of affairs is quite heated. You should train your self not to react.

By listening reflectively to each other, you're compelled to gradual down and assume rationally, that is critical if you need to avoid struggle with someone else and prevent any escalation of unwanted problem. When you keep to interrupt the tough man or woman, searching for to protect your self, or attack them for how they're being, you're now not responding thoughtfully however reacting mechanically, which isn't fine. With reflective listening, you want to be extra responsive, because of this you're more in control of your mind and emotions.

Learn to Ask Questions

Asking questions is vital to top off the gaps in verbal exchange and understanding.

When you pay attention reflectively, you may phrase that sure points may additionally additionally have lengthy beyond over your head, so the nice thing to do is ask questions to gain clarity. You can ask each an open-ended query or a close to-ended one. With the latter form of query, your answers can be yes or no, with out a similarly rationalization. Open-ended questions will often start with phrases like this:

Describe…

Explain…

What passed off…

How did…

Why did you…

What's the matter…

The splendid thing about open-ended questions is that you invite the alternative to provide their mindset. With close to-ended questions, you don't have some of contexts to work with from the solutions, however it gives you extra manage as the only asking the questions. The problem with close to-ended questions is that you will need to invite observe-up questions, which might not be the most green way to have a verbal exchange. A closed query like, "Would you need to take the lead in this?" have to give you either a superb or a no. However, asking the query, "How should you need to take the lead on this?" right now units up a scenario in which the opportunity man or woman can present their thoughts, and you may see the manner to art work with them as a cease result.

When asking questions, keep away from coming off as confrontational or rude. You don't want to be shielding and don't want them to marvel inside the event that they're on an episode of Law and Order with out their consent. Always ask the questions lightly and in a unbiased way even as speaking with a tough person so that you don't purpose them into being greater hard. Let them quit answering you in advance than you butt in with every different query. Sometimes it's difficult due to the fact their answer also can moreover inspire greater questions, however it's best to wait and permit them to make their factor earlier than you ask them some problem new. When they have got finished responding, it's beneficial to summarize or paraphrase the whole lot they said earlier than you give them your thing of view.

Questions and Emotions

When asking questions, it's a outstanding concept to discover how the opportunity character feels approximately a few element. You should ask them, "What are your thoughts in this count number?" or "How do you experience approximately this?" Asking what their emotions and thoughts are can will let you apprehend what it's far that's using them to act in an uncooperative way. Often, it helps humans to air their feelings earlier than you begin seeking out their cooperation on any rely. You need to create a connection with them, and there's no higher way to peer things via their eyes.

Just because of the fact you're seeing thru the opportunity man or woman's eyes doesn't endorse you have to truly discard your personal reviews and emotions to allow theirs take over your thoughts and heart. Your aim right proper right here is to understand how they see subjects, making it plenty less complicated in case you need to interact with them efficiently. Listen with the cause to enjoy subjects as they revel in them and to mirror their emotions decrease returned to them, even if you're now not going to attain this in terms.

If you've got interaction with difficult human beings efficaciously, you've were given to understand which you're now not usually going to percent the equal perspectives on troubles. This difference in values is the entire element in the back of active listening and its 3 elements; to help you see their element of view and show to them how crucial their angle is to you. Again, you don't need to don't forget them. You're clearly bridging the distance amongst you, displaying them which you're no longer going to chunk.

What You Say When You're Not Saying Anything

In addition to listening actively, you can gain masses from knowledge nonverbal verbal exchange. Effective communication isn't pretty heaps what is being stated however the way it's being stated. It's additionally approximately all the topics no longer being stated. Reading nonverbal verbal exchange can permit you to recognise loads more approximately the state of affairs you're in. Research has examined that nearly about feelings and emotions, a whopping 90 3 percentage of what's being communicated is nonverbal, with fifty 5 percentage of that being frame language and 38 percent the tone of voice. The actual words spoken notable account for 7 percentage. That way you can find out the proper that means of any communicated message in particular in what isn't being stated. You can tell if a person is involved, disgusted, sad, or irritated clearly from looking at their face and staring at their mannerisms. You can examine how they maintain or avoid eye contact, their posture, gesture, or sudden loss of gestures, and so on. Observing this stuff will permit you to recognize what they in fact revel in and if there's any congruence among their terms and their nonverbal communication.

When someone is having a difficult time speaking, their frame language will often end up more obvious. For instance, a person dissatisfied with you'll sound very quick and brusque. There are times at the same time as body language is hard to have a have a look at. For instance, you could anticipate a person standing with their hands on their hips is prepared to mission you, however that may not be the case. It may additionally really be their preferred posture for repute. The aspect is, it's now not clever to aspect out one gesture or facial abilties and anticipate that you recognize what the opportunity character is questioning or feeling. When it includes nonverbal communique, you must don't forget a mixture of factors as opposed to just one detail. The nonverbal signals from the opposite man or woman will frequently are available in clusters.

When you have got a cluster of body language and facial capabilities signals close to each different, you could anticipate they will have a story to tell you. So the extremely good way to interpret nonverbal conversation is to study most of these cues together. For example, a person can also moreover have crossed their arms at some point of their chest. Now, it'd be easy to expect they may be feeling shielding in case you truly checked out that one sign up its non-public. However, in case you check that they'll be additionally stamping their toes at the floor, you may recognize that they're truely bloodless.

Another issue to look out for is congruence, due to this you need to see if their nonverbal communication fits their verbal communique or now not. A loss of congruence is a splendid manner to be able to capture the passive-aggressive man or woman of their passive aggressiveness. Once you could see there may be no congruence among what they're pronouncing and the manner they're being, it's clean to be aware that they're now not being sincere with you. For example, you may ask a person to help you out with a mission, and they may say high-quality, they may. However, you will be aware that they're no longer looking you in the attention and seem to have slumped their shoulders, which suggests incongruence, as there may be no in shape among their verbal and nonverbal communication. This incongruence is also known as leakage. It's a few element that often takes place subconsciously, but you need to appearance out for it due to the truth in case you don't, you threat falling for lies.

Being able to study nonverbal indicators may be likened to the use of your instinct to study a situation. In this context, running together collectively together with your instinct is some aspect you do subconsciously as you respond to all of the nonverbal conversation you bought from a person else. When someone's lying to you, they typically rehearse what they're going to mention, however they don't think about how their our our bodies will act or betray them. So even as you have a look at that their frame is pronouncing some problem absolutely specific from what's popping out in their mouth, you could believe your intuition about now not getting the truth. To successfully take a look at nonverbal conversation, you want to attention on the information as well as the larger picture.

Teach Yourself to Read Others

An fantastic workout an wonderful manner to use to train yourself a manner to study others is to paintings together with your television. The next time you watch a show, placed the tv on mute and watch. You can also do that for records interviews. Pay interest to the manner people interact with every different. What are they doing with their our our bodies and faces? Unmute the TV after which pay attention to their tone of voice. In mild of what you've visible from the nonverbal verbal exchange, what are you getting from how they sound? What does your intuition assist you to know approximately their honesty? Are there clusters of behaviors you could put together the useful resource your thoughts? The more you exercise a manner to look at distinctive human beings, the better you'll be at handling tough situations that stand up.

One extra element you could do is be aware of human beings around you on the same time as ready in queues. You can also take a look at people on the coffee keep or on a bus. Try to bet what they're attempting to say to the alternative character. Pay hobby to the way the participants in the verbal exchange react to every different. Do they appear stressful or comfortable, or does their frame language advocate defensiveness? Is there leakage?

You must moreover be privy to your frame language. Whenever you're worried in an interplay, maintain in mind whether or not or no longer or now not your frame language is enhancing the scenario or making it worse. The odds are that you haven't idea approximately what you're communicating nonverbally until now. Even while you are saying not something, your body is pronouncing plenty. You can once in a while make a state of affairs worse with out even know-how it, which takes place even as you are pronouncing one issue, however your tone of voice or body language makes what you say seem disingenuous. For instance, you may be setting a clean boundary with someone, and they could interpret that as you threatening them.

Paying hobby in your body language makes it so you aren't probable to feed the terrible state of affairs and make it larger than it is. Mastering frame language does no longer advise which you have to research a bunch of recent gestures and poses that won't be just proper for you. Looking assured and spurring your thoughts and body to take a look at wholesome will display beneficial. Here's an high-quality time to make it easy that it is one element to seem confident and some other really to be virtually confident.

The following is a listing of things you could do to enhance how confident you enjoy.

Check your shoulders and ensure they're relaxed.

Speak slower.

Speak quieter.

Balance your body's weight frivolously on every legs.

Check your head and make sure it's degree.

Allow your elbows to rest at the arms of the chair even as you're taking a seat instead of keeping them tightly in competition in your aspects.

Engage in appropriate eye touch.

Sit right now.

Stand without delay.

Lower your voice pitch.

You don't want to do all of these items on the same time. Just or three of them are sufficient. Remember that you could't be 100% in control of all your nonverbal communication signs. So clearly, you handiest need three or of this stuff, and your emotions and mind will comply with wholesome.

There is a lot greater to interacting with difficult human beings than sincerely being attentive to them and asking them the proper questions. When you've got to permit a person understand that you're disenchanted with them, or they're a drain in your power, or you are not going to permit them to go your boundaries, you want to recognize what to say, how to say it, and whilst to mention it. It might be brilliant in case you observed out the way to be clean and honest at the same time as speaking your troubles with them. So in the following financial ruin, we are going to speak about assertive conversation.

Chapter 4: Be Assertive

When someone's being difficult, there are numerous techniques you could respond to their conduct. Admittedly, now not all of the responses are best. For example, you can have hassle remaining calm as you explicit your factor of view. Or, you could find it hard to be sincere and open about the manner you revel in. It is probably first rate if you placed a way to be assertive. In this manner, you could healthily reply to others with out resorting to strategies like screaming, being protective, blaming, or a few thing else.

What does it suggest to be assertive? It's the functionality to say what's genuinely in your mind. It's speakme what you need, want, experience, and bear in thoughts a few factor. It's fame up for what you receive as real with in although it makes you worried. You have a proper to precise yourself, so you must by no means allow others make you enjoy such as you shouldn't. As you stick up for your rights and values, it's essential to do not forget others. Think about their personal ideals and the manner they revel in. They additionally have their rights, and it's nicely really worth thinking about that while you're keeping yourself.

Some humans count on that being assertive is ready being a bully, but that's not the case. As you say your self, you encourage others to specific their perspectives. That way, you and the possibility character can trust each different, and you'll find it lots less complex to deal with some element disagreements you have got. The assertive individual is commonly inclined to negotiate, but they're furthermore company in their perspectives. It's all about stability. You get to pick the way you respond to the people spherical you due to the fact, as said earlier than, nobody makes you revel in or do a little aspect. Assertive humans might also moreover moreover rub some insecure people the wrong manner, but they live with their weapons at the same time as giving others the right to do the identical. Being assertive isn't approximately going into conversations seeking to "win" at the same time as the alternative man or woman loses.

Being Assertive in Practice

Spotting and Stating the Issue: To be assertive in a conversation, you first need to determine out precisely what the issue is after which say it out loud to the opportunity person. You need to pick out out most effective one hassle and no longer a myriad of them concurrently. Talking approximately the problem, be as precise as you could. Please don't expect the opportunity character is a thoughts reader and start losing pointers for them to try and artwork it out. Don't waste some time rambling or attempting to find to make excuses for what you enjoy. If you do, it's clean for the opportunity individual to dispose of the wrong message from what you sincerely intended.

When you're about to confront someone about a hassle, you may begin with the aid of telling them, "Hey, I'd like to talk with you about what occurred…." When speakme approximately the problem, avoid the temptation of listing all of the wrongs they have got carried out within the beyond. It might be superb in case you saved your interest squarely at the hassle. Also, be as brief as feasible, so you don't ramble on and on and lose your difficulty.

Say It as You Feel It: Once extra, we've set up that the alternative individual is not a mind reader. Therefore, it's miles important which you no longer most effective permit them to understand about the hassle but moreover the way you enjoy. Let the alternative person know which you're feeling irritated, upset, embarrassed, or whatever else. You ought to very very own what you experience. In one-of-a-kind words, in no way inform them, "You're making me sense like this." Remember, no individual makes you enjoy or perform a little component. So at the same time as you're talking about your feelings, you could say, "I experience indignant each time you do that." The specific man or woman has to apprehend how you enjoy so that they're now not blindsided.

The reason it's crucial to allow the other person apprehend the way you sense is simply so they will be consciously privy to the effect their movements are having on you. It also permits them recognize how essential it's far to clear up the problem.

Choosing to assault them through asking, "What the hell do you discovered you're doing?" or any question of that kind isn't really properly well worth it. Neither is attacking them thru pronouncing such things as "You're loopy." Here's a realistic instance of what it seems like to apprehend the problem and nation your feelings.

"Darren, I want to speak to you approximately what takes location when you carry site visitors domestic with out letting me recognize in advance of time. Last night time time time, while to procure right here domestic with Mark and Louise, I wasn't searching ahead to them. I'd made dinner for simply you, me, and the kids, and I had to scramble to conjure a few problem up in your pals to eat. That made me experience tired, and I actually have grow to be frustrated and disappointed."

Own Your Part inside the Problem: This is the element in which you need to maintain in thoughts that your values do now not constantly align with those of others. So in region of accusing the alternative character of being wrong, you want to renowned the manner you moreover may additionally performed a feature in growing the problem. For instance, I need to admit; I didn't whinge the final time it passed off, so you also can furthermore have notion it became ok. Or, I admit I acted like the entirety changed into splendid.

Be Clear about What You Want or Don't Want: Now that you have famous your component and the hassle, you need to be clean about what you need or no longer want to arise. You can't skip this step due to the fact if you do, you've taken all of the issues and placed them on the alternative character's shoulders. In our make-trust situation, you could want Darren to will permit you to recognize a day or earlier than inviting pals over to the residence. Alternatively, you could need to make clear that you'll no longer make dinner for buddies who come over unannounced. Whatever you need, you need to be as quick and concise as feasible. Leave no room for guessing on the other character's element through being particular. They're likely to forget while you ramble after making your elements, and so do you. You don't want to make numerous excuses. All you want is a fantastic motive why you could favor to do or no longer do some thing. State what you need after which phrase how they respond.

Hear Them Out and Acknowledge Their Answer: After letting the alternative man or woman recognize the problem, sit up for them to talk. If they're no longer volunteering, you may spark off them with a query like, "What do you sense about this?" Getting a solution out of them shows them which you care approximately their reviews and also you're now not simply trying to manipulate or bully them into doing a little element you want. At this factor, it is critical to exercise lively listening. It may be excellent in case you were now not listening with the motive to correct or interrupt them earlier than they've finished.

Remember, earlier than responding to their answer; you should make sure that you're each at the identical web page and understand them successfully. Once greater, there is no need an amazing manner to roll over and take transport of as proper with something they say. You want to apprehend in which they're coming from. Acknowledge what they say via repeating it in a unique way. When you respond, make certain you direct your hobby satisfactory to the applicable factors. Be aware approximately letting your anger or aggression take over you because the immediately you do, the possibility individual's attention moves from what you're announcing in your mind-set. So as you talk with them, ensure that your voice is impartial and relaxed. Also, hold the temptation to whine in test. If you find out yourself giving in to the urge to break, express regret and tell them they ought to hold. Continue to renowned and respond to their answers.

Know How to Stick Up for You: Sometimes, in the center of a confrontation, the opportunity individual will deliver up a factor that has not anything to do with the issue available. If you word you're getting distracted, it could be due to the truth you're letting the possibility character take charge of the conversation. If no matter your notable efforts, it seems the possibility character isn't paying interest, or they're operating to sidetrack you, you can prevent this with the aid of the usage of the use of constantly sticking for your critical element. Continue to copy your point as flippantly as you can till they select to widely known it.

Some tough people are very foxy in their tries to get you off trouble count. Some of them are downright competitive. Regardless of the methods, they are in search of to use closer to you. You mustn't launch a counterattack. You need to do your awesome no longer to whine, sulk or supply in to their tries to get you sidetracked. Respond to them to permit them to apprehend you've stated what they're saying. However, you are sticking to the factor at hand. Let's anticipate Darren makes the component which you've allowed his friends to go back over and in no manner complained approximately it within the beyond. Don't respond with the aid of saying "I understand that I by no means complained approximately your pal coming over late within the beyond. However, ought to you attention on what befell the day before today?"

Be Open to Negotiation and Compromise: When the selection gives itself, you need to be willing to barter with the other person or at the least gain a compromise. Your mind should be on the hunt for opportunity solutions. For example, you may endorse to Darren, "How approximately the subsequent time your buddies come over, you put together them some pizza?" Nothing should rely more to you at this aspect than looking for commonplace ground. The exceptional way you can each negotiate is if you've expressed your views absolutely to each different. The cool detail approximately negotiating and compromising is that the other person can't get so upset that they not take note of what you're pronouncing. Neither do you get so labored up that you could't interest on fixing things. The important trouble is to arrive at an answer that works for both of you. So be easy about your limits and barriers, and don't allow the opportunity individual to pass them due to the fact you are attempting to negotiate.

Figuring Out Solutions

Before you have interplay in a verbal exchange with a hard character, you have to bear in mind what it is that you need and what limits you'll no longer permit them to push you to. Here are a few useful questions you could ask yourself before you engage on this verbal exchange.

What do I want?

What don't I want?

What do I want this individual to do?

What do I need this individual not to do?

What compromises am I inclined to make?

What are my limits?

What remarkable alternatives do I virtually have if the opposite person refuses to artwork with me?

When considering the manner ahead, you want to make sure you're no longer thinking about punishing or threatening the opposite character. When you threaten the opposite individual, the chances are they're now not going to want to paintings with you to find out a solution. Threats can also lead you every to lose your cool, and that may be negative to the final results you've got been hoping to gather. So maintain your thoughts centered on solutions. That manner, you may have severa alternatives even though the opposite man or woman doesn't want to cooperate with you.

If it seems the opportunity person is refusing to cooperate, you need to not waste a while taking into account strategies to get even. The important problem to do is recall the effects. As you try this, you may apprehend logical results. There might be outcomes regardless of what the alternative man or woman makes a selection to do. For example, if Darren refuses to save you bringing his pals with the aid of the use of so late for dinner, the effect might be that you now not prepare dinner for them. Remember, you have to now not threaten the other man or woman. So you don't have to tell them what the outcome in their choice may be. You can quietly determine that you're not cooking late-night time time time meals.

If you insist on explaining what's going to take location if the opportunity character does no longer cooperate, you need to be prepared for the way they will react to that. They may additionally determine to get irritated with you, or they may decide to get petty or perhaps. There are constantly outcomes for standing up on your rights and limitations. There may be instances while subjects pass wrong, and also you don't assume them to. In times like those, you don't have the distance or potential to bear in mind answers or the way ahead. Rather than allow your feelings to weigh down you sincerely, it is proper to inform the opportunity character that you need some area and time to count on via the trouble. You can come decrease lower back and function a hard communique even as you determine it out.

Considering answers and consequences is an great way to cope with difficult human beings to your existence because it forces you to artwork collectively along with your logical mind. You're now not prone to the outbursts that might come due to being emotional. When humans engage in a confrontational communique and start to hassle threats, this occurs because such some of emotions are worried. Where emotions rule, it's far tough to stay cool and rational. So as you've got interplay with the humans to your lifestyles, it might be satisfactory in case you idea approximately answers and effects because of the fact that puts you inside the using pressure's seat. You're the one who entails a selection in case you're going to make any modifications and the manner you will permit subjects play out if the opportunity individual refuses to cooperate.

Chapter 5: What To Do When You're Attacked

In nowadays's society, anger and hostility are on the rise. More and more people appear to be taking their anger out on others. The growth in hostility is probable because of progressed publicity to violence within the media, in which humans see it time and again appear without being able to save you it. Regardless of why hostility has advanced, what are you capable of do about it?

Hostility hurts relationships with own family members, pals, and coworkers. It can purpose physical assault or maybe demise if left unchecked. It can be terrifying to need to cope with someone who's being unfavorable. People get competitive because of the fact they need to manipulate and dominate the situation to get what they need. Another cause they act in this manner is that they'll be responding to a few thing they think will take region to them or some element that's already took place. The first and 2d reasons for their reaction are instrumental aggression and impulsive aggression, respectively.

People who resort to instrumental aggression have discovered out a while lower again that they are capable of get what they need from others every time they may be difficult. For those human beings, hostility and aggression aren't certainly fueled thru manner of emotion. It's all a show for them to get what they need from you. However, simply because it's obsessed on show or they only want some element out of you doesn't suggest that aggression doesn't have very actual consequences on you and your psyche. That character is performing as a bully.

When you're interacting with someone, and they pick out out impulsive aggression, it's frequently because they've got a want that is not met, and so they will revel in disappointed or wronged. For the ones humans, their anger may also furthermore make the effort to construct. At other instances even though, some thing need to reason them and cause them to indignant all of a unexpected. Whether you're dealing with impulsive or instrumental aggression, every situation can leave you emotionally dysregulated. However, even within the face of hostility, there are procedures on the manner to make sure your emotions don't get the amazing of you. Active listening will help you considerably here. So will being assertive.

When managing a antagonistic man or woman, you may permit them to manage the scenario, interact with them, or stroll far from the war of words. It might be nice in case you remembered that anything hassle they've is theirs and not your burden to endure. You are first-rate to be held responsible for your alternatives of moves. Their moves and emotions are not your duty. When coping with aggressive human beings, it is crucial that you are very capable of dealing with your personal anger and which you are a sturdy individual. If you don't do this, you open yourself as a lot as being attacked extra regularly. Depending on the manner you respond, you can make the scenario higher or worse. Choose to react with boldness, and that lets in them to understand which you aren't one to be bullied. Your body is a useless giveaway as to the way you're feeling, so endure in mind the confident actions we listed within the preceding bankruptcy, and make certain to do at least or 3 of them. As you perform these actions, you can be conscious that your body and thoughts observe in form, even inside the face of hostility.

The Challenge

Assume for a 2d which you've virtually been advised off by using manner of someone who usually isn't aggressive. At that 2nd, it's easy to experience damage. It additionally can be pretty complicated because of the truth this person is normally quite affordable. They just had a demanding day and lashed out at the closest person, which took place to be you. When compelled, how they generally interact with others may be quite intimidating, so it's hard for all and sundry to mission them. Despite this issue, you need to recall that in case you do no longer mission them for his or her behavior, there is no way they may change. You can great get up to them if you have the self guarantee to tell them how they're able to or can not act in the direction of you. Rather than allow your nerves get to you, you have to cope with human beings like this regardless of your fears. In unique terms, it's k to be afraid, however you want to get up to them and explicit your troubles.

One element to maintain in thoughts is whether or not or no longer or not or not some element approximately you encourages them to behave this way. Perhaps you look like the weakest individual to them, so it's easy for them to cope with you the way they do. If this is the case, the answer isn't a good manner to try to please them. The solution doesn't lie in rolling over and taking all their insults or making your self ingratiated to them. Keeping your lips sealed doesn't help the state of affairs each. The intention is with a view to permit them to apprehend together with your terms what you need and what you don't want out of your interactions.

Practical Solution

Figure out the Problem: Did the hard person in query criticize you unfairly or yell at you? Could or no longer it's miles that they're now not being attentive to what you're pronouncing and interrupting you? Before you address them, you need to get your self clean approximately the problem. Ask yourself what you didn't like approximately the interaction you both had. Also, discern out what your limits and barriers are. Then the onus is on you to allow them to recognize what you need or don't need. You must get comfortable with telling them your thoughts as they will be. Let's anticipate that your boss gave you commands to carry out a venture. You ask them to make clean a few factor, simplest for them to yell "I've already told you!" Your herbal inclination is probably to attack them or to lessen. A lots higher technique might be to lightly reply to them via pronouncing "I would decide upon it in case you counseled me again in preference to yelling at me." If they respond thru manner of pronouncing, "Don't be stupid, I didn't yell at you." you can say "I'm not being silly. Could you please offer an purpose for another time?" If you find a few sarcasm of their voice, you could ask them, "Could you inform me exactly what you need, please?" If this character maintains interrupting, you wait till they've stated what they want to mention and then reply, "I want to complete what I become announcing before."

Beginning with "I" Rather than "You": Would you want to understand the quickest way to get someone at the protecting? Begin your sentences with the word "You." This, of direction, is a horrible idea. Saying things like "You in no way pay hobby!" or "You're continuously distracted!" will revel in like an assault at the opportunity person, and if you want to reason them to become protective in place of listening to you out. It might be incredible in case you didn't lodge to blaming because of the truth a very good manner to not remedy subjects. Do your first rate to hold yourself responsible for your mind and feelings. Don't reduce your self to insults. Just permit them to understand how you enjoy and what you'll or acquired't stand for, but acquire this with out degrading them, in any other case they'll meet you with stiff competition.

Pick the Right Time and Place: There are effective conditions at the same time as it's now not appropriate to offer the alternative character a reaction right away. For instance, there can be splendid folks who do now not want to be aware of your communique. Or you'll be too beaten thru your emotions to deal with the problem appropriately. In times like the ones, you need to wait till you've got the right conditions to talk to the opportunity person. However, you don't need to attend too lengthy. Things might also worsen amongst you . So cope with it as quickly as you could.

Hear them out, deliver a reaction, however maintain your ground:

1.   Once more, maintain in thoughts to live impartial and calm as you talk.

2.   Don't supply the difficult character any shape of hostility to latch onto as an excuse to be even more hard in the direction of you. You may not always get the very last outcomes you decide upon all the time, however that shouldn't prevent you.

3. Continue to be assertive for your responses. Eventually, the alternative person receives the message.

Another Challenge

What do you do on the identical time as you're handling a tough or irritated patron, and you're not the most effective liable for anything has disappointed them? If they're channeling their anger closer to you, it's very easy so you can lose your cool and end up as irrational as they may be. However, it might be top notch in case you recollect that they may be indignant, because of this that they cannot count on or speak rationally within the advise time. Unless this person is bodily or emotionally attacking you, you may't inform them to move away and go again once they feel higher. In this case, you need to deal with the trouble there and then. You're not the problem in this case except you're the only who made a mistake, of direction. Even if their anger is a give up end result of some mistakes you made, you're now not chargeable for how they experience on the stop of the day. So please don't take at the burden of being chargeable for their responses. Your purpose in this situation is to pay attention to them, renowned their plight and the way they sense, and provide a functionality solution.

Practical Solution

Listen Reflectively: Reflective listening is an super way to defuse their anger because of the fact the opposite person can see that you are listening to how they revel in and what they assume. It is useful to permit the entirety out at the same time as people are irritated, so do not interrupt them. If you are saying a few component in advance than they've completed, you're honestly going to make a awful scenario worse. When they have got completed talking with you, allow them to realise which you've heard and understood the entirety they've said.

Negotiate and Compromise: Whenever you may, you want to make a point of negotiating with the opportunity individual and imparting an answer as a compromise. It's no longer the proper detail to do to be aware of someone who's irritated and impolite. However, figuring out which you're going to live unbiased and awesome is a exceptional manner to place out the flames. Also, with the resource of method of choosing to be great, you are graciously permitting the possibility individual the opportunity to take it down a notch and be affordable and respectful. You are allowing them to hold face, which is a high-quality trouble.

One More Challenge

Let's count on you are using thru site visitors for your way to an appointment with a patron. You all at once observe that there's a using stress who's tailgating you. This riding force is impolite and making angry gestures at you, this is a bit frightening. Where you're not approximately to offer in and permit them to win, you do the great component you could take into account. You try to breathe thru it, determined no longer to permit the purpose pressure pass. Next problem you recognize, the motive force in the back of you has overtaken you, and that they did so in a manner that forced you off the road to preserve your self.

In this case, the obligation lies each with you and the using force. On the simplest hand, it's no longer your fault that the driving pressure have become so careless on the road. Road rage is clearly inexcusable irrespective of how past due you're or wherein you're going. On the alternative hand, you've got been determined to ensure they didn't get their way. Inevitably, this introduced approximately the state of affairs turning into worse. It might be a miles better possibility no longer to allow the the use of pressure get even angrier than he already changed into. Your purpose is to remedy this case and to remain as calm as possible to stay stable on the road.

Practical Solution

Stay Passive: The fine issue you may do is to mention actually not anything, despite the fact that they're yelling at you. Please don't slump to their degree. Ensure which you keep your eyes on the street in advance of you. As brief as you're succesful, allow them to overtake you and circulate on. While drivers with road rage may be worrying, the important component even as using is to live secure, so that you don't need to get engaged in a physical or verbal altercation. Check your pride.

A Final Note on Dealing with Hostility

When handling an unmistakably adverse individual, you need to understand they're normally equipped for a combat. So, you've were given to be tactful and characteristic the strength to deal with the situation. It is probably high-quality if you had tact because of the truth you don't need to purpose them to angrier than they already are. But it's furthermore appropriate in case you had energy because of the reality you don't need them to count on you're prone or without problems manipulated. The hassle have become handling adverse human beings is that even as you could recognize the proper factor to do is to stay calm, their electricity may be quite infectious. Next factor you understand, you begin to experience irritated, dissatisfied and harassed about why you're in this situation. Your project at all times is to make sure you and the alternative character's feelings don't get the better of you. No rely how horrible matters can also additionally appear, there's usually a way to behave with out feelings clouding your judgment. The following is a listing of guidelines for what you can do at that 2nd:

Be clean on what it's far the opposite individual has a hassle with.

Figure out what they need.

Figure out what they don't need.

Be clear about the quantity of hostility you will or acquired't tolerate.

Acknowledge the validity of the alternative character's emotions and point of view.

Think approximately solutions and compromises.

Listen to them, renowned their responses, and stay business organization while vital.

Adopt postures, expressions, and body indicators that make you appear confident.

Here's a listing of factors to keep away from doing:

Don't interrupt.

Don't launch a counterattack.

Don't abuse them or use insulting words.

Don't blame.

Don't disgrace.

Don't get defensive.

Don't wait spherical in case you feel it's no longer stable to be within the same location with them.

Chapter 6: How To Deal With A Passive Aggressive

It may be very frustrating even as you're handling someone who isn't immediately letting you apprehend they're upset. Often, it's not apparent why those human beings act the way they do. They do their excellent to preserve their actual motives hidden from you. When you decide to name them out, they act like not anything goes on, and also you're the crazy one seeing matters that aren't there.

For maximum people, when confronted with a passive-competitive individual, the default reaction is to avoid them or reduce away. However, this is not a feasible tactic whilst it's a person you can't keep away from, like a colleague at art work or a member of the family. It doesn't assist to distance yourself all the time or definitely reduce off someone residing with you under the same roof. When you have to connect with those humans often, being tolerant of their conduct only encourages them to preserve going, and it may get even worse. So you have to get equipped to confront them and realize it's now not going to be clean. You'll need to live grounded inside the route of the alternate if you're going to get them to come again clean approximately what's taking place. They will hold to throw one excuse after some other or stay reticent of their replies. When you maintain with the proper method, they'll haven't any desire but to provide in and speak the truth.

Staying calm after they're not being sincere will help you deduce the problem, and then you can work on crafting an answer for you every. Instead of strolling to change the way they're appearing, bear in mind the way you respond instead. You're the most effective who receives to dictate how the relationship is going for the reason that they're no longer being cooperative. Let's look at the manner to be assertive and lead the possibility person in which you need them to go.

A Challenge

Imagine you've been assigned to paintings on a project with a tough, passive-competitive individual. You've had to deal with this man or woman within the beyond. This man or woman made a factor of continuously capturing down your mind whilst offering little in the way of options. He changed into moreover intentionally incompetent, showing up overdue and doing some aspect he need to to frustrate you with the aid of doing something however what you each agreed. His actions made you experience very stressed out, and your self perception took a success, so the remaining component you want to do is should work with this man or woman. You even tried to speak with them approximately their behavior, but they were dismissive.

There's now not whatever more infuriating than assuming you and a person are at the same thing or have agreed to something only to find out they have got their very private time table. The person does something that pushes you right right into a sticky state of affairs, and their attitude at the ground must recommend they're clueless approximately what they've completed. However, you may inform that they have been being disingenuous, and they meant to undermine you. Regardless of who this individual is, whether or now not they're a pal, a colleague, or a lover, in case you pick out to confront them, they're simply going to offer you excuse after excuse, at the way to go away you even extra pissed off.

Is there any manner you'll be contributing to this difficult state of affairs? Possibly.

Whenever a person does something to undermine you or marvel you in a terrible manner, every so often it's because of the truth you didn't permit them to be easy about what they preferred or didn't want. They can also moreover have attempted to talk up, but you weren't paying interest. It may be that you didn't take a look at in with them to make certain they had been good sufficient with the preparations you made and truly assumed they had been pinnacle with the whole thing. The purpose of this project is to expose them it's adequate to be sincere approximately what they need, to reiterate what you're each in agreement about, and to get them to stick to the plan.

Practical Solution

If this individual has completed a few thing off script to area you in a tough area, you can before everything have no concept a way to reply to their movements. You may additionally additionally need to lash out, speak up about how you're irritated, or permit them to guide via mirroring their passive aggressiveness. None of these techniques are useful. If you lash out at them, they'll each deny what you're announcing, be sarcastic, or play the victim. They may additionally keep to push the bounds with their passive aggressiveness, and subsequent difficulty, you're every reenacting scenes from Tom and Jerry as you attempt to get lower returned at each unique. This combat is a waste of time and electricity.

When confronting this individual, please don't spend any time attempting to reveal you're proper and they're incorrect. There's additionally no need to element out the facts about the agreed direction of motion you each had. Whatever you do, don't accuse them, and don't begin sentences with "you" due to the fact on the way to most effective motive them to shielding, and also you obtained't make headway with them. Use "I" sentences rather, and fine usa the information of the state of affairs. For example, you may tell them, "I became greatly surprised through…" or "I have grow to be careworn even as…." Instead of confronting them head-on, remember what you've discovered from what honestly occurred and the way you may do subjects in a special way in order that they don't feel the want to undermine you next time. Let's study realistic steps you could soak up this situation.

Find out what they need or don't want thru the usage of active listening: Ask them for his or her input the use of open questions. For example, you could ask How might you want to preserve? It doesn't rely if their answer isn't easy sufficient. You want their answer as a basis you could assemble some issue strong on. So, whilst handling this colleague, it's viable that they'll have provided you thoughts within the beyond, but you weren't paying interest for a few motive. Whenever you're talking with this character (and absolutely everyone else, honestly), generally take a look at in with your self to make certain you're allowing them to specific their opinion. Usually, humans surprise you with underhanded, shady behavior due to the fact they get the feel that their opinion is not valued. So, that is an opportunity for you to expose them the manner to be assertive and direct approximately what they need.

If you study the opposite person has no concept what to mention in response on your query or appears reluctant, you may begin providing solutions to them. The difference now is that you will ask what they think about the answers you're providing. Ask them in the occasion that they think a few factor's going to paintings or now not, and if the latter is the case, ask them what they count on might be a better opportunity. You need to apply open inquiries to get them to open up. It's additionally fine to offer them the choice of doing now not whatever because of the fact every now and then they don't want to accomplish that but don't recognize the way to speak that. Always listen to them actively and well known the whole lot they may be pronouncing. It is probably remarkable if you continually stored the desire to artwork with them at the vanguard of your mind as you engage with them because it will allow them to be sincere approximately what they want.

Chapter 7: The 10 Annoying Human Characteristics

We all have many contradictions. We are what we're due to that. Fun, too and now not amusing. Interaction styles or persona inclinations range substantially. Here are arguably the pinnacle 10, which have been culled from some of lists, studies, and interactions with hundreds of people.

1.   Being a company in doom.

Are you continuously pessimistic? "Yes... BUT," do you find out yourself pronouncing that? Do you throw ice water on extraordinary human being's thoughts, schemes, or aspirations? Even in case you keep in mind yourself to be realistic or realistic, being round a person who only sees the horrible factors of things may be difficult. Maybe it is time to reduce your use of "but"?

2. Complaining (approximately the whole thing)

Being a doom supplier is not what this is approximately because of the reality that that is all about you, not the relaxation of the area. Nothing is ever proper—your artwork, your boss, your companion, your children, your busy schedule, your existence. Why were you treated so unfairly? Although you could lead a hard life, is there a way you could use some time and energy greater wisely? Maybe you'll likely every now and then turn your hobby outward and ask human beings how they may be doing?

3. Have to be proper all of the time.

Do you experience being the last to speak? To repeatedly strength a factor home till all of us is happy or you've humiliated them? You are definitely clever, and you can regularly be correct, however are you moreover may moreover silly? Do the people you have have been given been the usage of your brilliance to brainwash require a sleep and a double dosage of panadol in a while? Why do you sense the need to be right all the time? Why not try being curious as an possibility?

four. Disrupting high-quality people.

Do you speak eventually of various people's speeches? Do you continually have a COOL(ER) story to characteristic ALWAYS? Wait your turn. You is probably funnier or more thrilling than the character speaking, or you may have a ton of thrilling tales to proportion. Give others a hazard, specially the greater reserved ones. When you interrupt with but each extraordinary captivating information approximately yourself, it's truely rude. There have to now not be a proper away route once more to you.

5.   Constant self-advertising

Most people also can advantage from having more self belief, that could be a amazing element. But regular self-advertising wears humans out. It's all regular or even healthy in case you do it sometimes, however what in case you constantly compete for hobby? One extra selfie, please? Hmmm.

6.   Scattershot attention.

In contemporary-day disturbing society, that is EXTREMELY not unusual. Are you someone who has trouble specializing of their art work? Or the individual you're speaking to? Or lots of some aspect? Even if you can accomplish a lot, you also are telling absolutely everyone else that they're nicely virtually really worth a good deal much less than the content material cloth you truly glanced through on your phone. You can give an explanation for it away as worry or a focal point trouble, however you may encounter as uninformed, uncaring, and dismissive. Do you definitely want that?

7. Unreliability.

Do you have a information of canceling plans at the final minute or failing to expose up at events? Or do you want to consider all of your alternatives right now so that you can decide it virtually is extraordinary? Even on the identical time as you may enjoy like you're making clever options, you're certainly (quietly) teaching distinctive humans a manner to address you. So do no longer take it in my view if others begin to distance themselves from you or exclude you from fun sports activities sports. Instead, paintings on making guarantees and preserving them, especially to the folks that keep in mind.

8. Constantly being overdue.

The stylish hassle of being fashionably overdue might also additionally additionally have as soon as existed, however it has because of the fact outlived its usefulness. Most humans do not have enough time, that may be a precious commodity. People will genuinely recognize your tardiness as impolite and disrespectful until you're notably essential or renowned. Consider the message that being continuously overdue sends to extraordinary human beings: that they're now not critical sufficient which will charge their time. Moreover, which you lack commercial enterprise organization and are unprepared.

9. Being silly (take the stupid test).

It may be a quit result of introversion, shyness, social anxiety, or mild despair to in no manner do (or suggest some difficulty). BUT it would in addition be called not trying. Okay if no man or woman devices and you pick out out spending the weekend curled up on the sofa. Don't count on the road to form out of doors your door, despite the fact that, in case your passivity extends to never taking part with the out of doors international, not being in in any respect revolutionary or worried, and, in particular, now not surely disturbing about people. It's likely remarkable which you do now not care due to the truth else it may not.

10. Aggressive behavior this is passive.

Okay, this will probably spoil relationships. It's greater than absolutely bothersome. When we act as even though the whole thing is nicely however underneath we are hurting, we lash out in diffused ways like muttered insults, sullen or defiant conduct, or purposefully failing to carry out duties. Beware if you have this propensity due to the fact you run the threat of jeopardizing your vital relationships. Try to recognize whilst some issue irritates you and be extra forthright at the same time as addressing it

Chapter 8: How To Grow Your Empathy For A Difficult Person

It's tempting to keep away from someone as a good buy as feasible once they irritate you at paintings. But doing so isn't always possible and often makes topics worse. It may be higher in order to increase some empathy. How are you purported to try this with a coworker that irritates you? How are you able to encourage inquiry in location of hostility?

Everyone has come across someone at paintings who annoys them,

It may be because of the manner this man or woman communicates, or in all likelihood it is due to the truth he well-knownshows disrespectful actions, like arriving late for meetings. But in a time at the same time as the place of business is turning into extra agency-orientated and obligations often name for near cooperation, you need to find a method to connect and forge a relationship with even the maximum obnoxious human beings. It's a splendid idea to begin via growing compassion for those styles of coworkers, no matter how tough they'll be. When managing hard humans, you may maintain a rational and well-calibrated attitude through the usage of empathy. Here are some hints.

1. Reflect

To begin with, recollect that your coworker is not intentionally in search of to get under your pores and pores and pores and skin. More often than not, they'll be responding to activities in their lives. Depersonalize the trouble and take a near have a study your self. Having self-awareness and a deep records of our private mental make-up strengthens your capability for empathy. After all, cultivating compassion — both self-compassion and compassion for others is your primary purpose. When a person is using you loopy, it helps to ask yourself, "What's causing me to react this way?" Your frustration may not continuously be about that person in any respect, it might be approximately you. Perhaps your colleague or boss reminds you of a person else you do not like.

2. Be composed

When your coworker arrives past due, interrupts you, or is without a doubt being obnoxious, you could experience a physiological response. Recognize the symptoms and signs that you're getting brought on. Maybe your breath accelerates, your fingers start to sweat, or your temperature rises. Giving in to the ones symptoms and signs and symptoms risks "amygdala hijack," in which you lose get admission to to the rational, thinking a part of your mind. Instead, take a few deep breaths.

three. Be observant

When you're disenchanted or indignant, each of the two sorts of empathy— cognitive empathy, that is the capacity to understand another person's angle, and emotional empathy, it genuinely is the functionality to experience every exclusive man or woman's feelings have a tendency to shut down.

What motivates this man or woman? "What excites and conjures up him?" Look beyond your very private worldview and don't forget what may be in his cultural historic beyond, schooling, own family state of affairs, or every day pressures it is inflicting him to behave like that.

To deal with a person who irritates you, you night time time need to strive picturing them as a six-year-vintage; in unique phrases, keep in mind that they're most effective human. The hypotheses you generated to offer an explanation for your colleague's behavior may be beneficial right right here; probably this man or woman is harassed or underneath stress, or possibly this individual is really not having a superb day. You do not need to come to be their pal.

four. Think to your Similarities

Instead of focusing in your differences, search for the similarities you percentage. Start small. Perhaps you and your colleague have youngsters the equal age. Maybe your colleague lives in a network or city which you recognize in element. Use the ones connections to strike up a verbal exchange. If all else fails, riff off an exchange you each seemed to discover a laugh.

five. Be sympathetic

The fact is which you have a tendency to offer people you want the advantage of the doubt, which makes it less complex so that you can revel in sympathetic toward them. You often expect the worst while interacting with someone you do not like, and this thoughts-set manifests in your conduct. Try to stop that response by means of way of using doing or announcing some component kind. Offer to assist with a assignment or reward the person on a suggestion they made at a meeting. But it ought to not be pressured. It ought to be genuine. Let's take the example of your colleague arriving late in your weekly crew assembly again and again. Avoid grumbling or sneering. Also, chorus from the use of passive-aggressive language consisting of, "Nice of you to enroll in us." Although it is probably your intuition, resist it. Say some thing like "Welcome" in its area. Before you take a seat down down down, get a cup of coffee, and we're going to get you on pinnacle of factors. This form of spirit of generosity is powerful to each you and your coworker. And maintain in thoughts that you usually have the choice to select empathy.

Chapter 9: Taking Control Of Your Own Difficult Behavior

Most probably, taken into consideration certainly one of your coworkers in reality dislikes some of your behavior. When you look at this, you may experience numerous emotions, in conjunction with humiliation, disbelief, rage, and disgrace. To deal with the state of affairs gently and logically, but, attempt to refrain from reacting adversely and make use of the subsequent techniques:

1. Empathize: Ask the other individual to offer an cause of what has indignant him so you could possibly attempt to understand the situation from his issue of view. For instance, you can sense that expressing your advocate to two coworkers within the middle in their conversation is beneficial, however if you try this regularly, you'll probably growth a recognition for "butting in."

2. Observe your body language: Do you ever have the impact that a person is truly not pleased with you? She hasn't said something at once, but there's a nagging sense that some factor is off. Nonverbal cues like a person's tone of voice, sighs, eye rolls, shrugs, or folded hands can recommend that they do not like what you're doing or pronouncing. If this takes vicinity, bear in thoughts expressing your willingness to talk about the problem with others through way of making use of open body language and voice tone.

3. Remain tremendous: Realize that walking to exchange your behavior may additionally additionally want to enhance your everyday usual overall overall performance and relationships together with your crew. Your popularity and assignment development will probably advantage from this.

Complaints do now not have to be private jabs; actually ask yourself, "Is this honest?" So, if you anticipate a coworker is appearing aggressively or that his feedback are unjustified, be assertive. If hard him makes you uncomfortable, specially if he's your boss, ask HR for steering or, if suitable, a sincere peer.

four. Use introspection: You can decide whether or not or now not you are appearing in a manner that is respectful of and high-quality in your venture with the useful resource of truly evaluating your non-public behavior. Unknowingly, you may have engaged in dangerous, complacent, or lazy moves which can be negatively affecting the ones round you. Set a remarkable example and regulate your walking style if this is the case. Let's take a look at a case take a look at from interactions with humans in fact going through hard human beings at artwork

Case Study #1: Be considerate and perceptive of your colleague's perspective

According to Bentley University President Gloria Larson, empathy for other humans comes surely to her. She explains, "I became frequently the ultra-modern infant in college developing up as an Air Force brat. I had to continuously learn how to like and get to understand oldsters who've been very one-of-a-type from me.

Her ability for empathy has been examined over the path of an prolonged profession. Gloria oversaw the improvement of the Massachusetts Convention Center, a $800 million waterfront production mission, decrease returned while she practiced regulation in Boston.

Another board member named Paul (not his real name) had a completely hard demeanor. Gloria believed he became destructive the paintings of the opportunity board contributors thru using liberating statistics to the media. Gloria, however, changed into determined not to permit Paul win. "If a person irritates me, I exit of my manner to get to realise them and like them."

Gloria taken into consideration Paul's functionality driving forces. She attempted kindness as an alternative, "but I didn't spend too much time thinking about that - I did not need to project." "I gave him a drink invitation,"

Gloria maintained an open, composed posture in the direction of the entire chat. Her aim have turn out to be to speak approximately the project similarly to get to apprehend Paul for my part. Instead of accusing Paul of leaking, she talked about their shared goal of "finding a way to get this mission over the quit line."

Gloria decided extra about Paul's perspectives at the project during their communicate. He changed into concerned that our actions might publicly denigrate the previous management, she remembers.

Gloria's expertise of Paul's arguments turned into really a revelation to Paul as properly. "I actually have end up conscious that I needed to tone down my public criticism of the preceding manipulate. And I don't forget he understood that we did not want to be adversaries. We have to cooperate."

Case Study #2: Put extra strive into studying more approximately your colleague's facts

When running with a hard coworker, Sandra Slager, chief strolling officer at MindEdge, a web analyzing platform for businesses and institutions, says she constantly reminds herself to "assume the tremendous" approximately that person. She says, "I attempt to hold in thoughts that he's no longer intentionally making me insane."

She likewise attempts to be grounded. I apprehend that operating with a person effectively could no longer require that I like them.

Several years ago, Sandra and Louis had been tasked with working on a piece of writing mission (now not his real name). She recollects that "he changed into so scared and agitated out," and that this pressure "came out in his snapping at me and performing like a bully."

Sandra changed into conscious that motion modified into required. Although she confesses it wasn't constantly out of the goodness of her coronary heart, she concedes that growing empathy for Louis have become a logical first step. "I wasn't genuinely brought on thru altruism once I decided directly to be sympathetic. It have turn out to be an attempt to find out a way to my predicament of the way to cooperate with him.

Louis advised her he had been sacked from his previous employment for a few component that wasn't his fault, and she or he or he made a special effort to get to recognize him and "recognize his beyond." She moreover decided that Louis grow to be the daddy of adolescent youngsters who were finishing university applications.

She explains, "He emerge as concerned approximately his family's properly-being and his livelihood due to the reality the activity changed into so crucial to him. Knowing these items, I end up better able to recognize him and the supply of his pressure.

Sandra changed into extra sympathetic toward Louis' frazzled nerves. She attempted her outstanding to reassure him about her contribution to the strive. We both desired this concept to achieve achievement, I assured him. Additionally, she keeps, "we each needed to recall each other to perform our components successfully.

Working with Louis changed with time, turning into "much less of an emotional strive and extra of a technical project," in line with her. Although our desires have been comparable, our styles were not.

The task became correctly completed. Louis and Sandra have collaborated on some of projects inside the course of the years. He's though stressed out, but we get along well at artwork.

Chapter 10: Dealing With Difficult People In Conflict

Sometimes the try among you and the difficult person can get to a point which could in all likelihood cease end result to war. You don't want to be instructed, the anxiety a number of the each of you may get to an alarming rate that's clearly volatile. Let's test few strategies to treatment that.

1.   Avoid Being Hooked!!!

It's referred to as a "Hook" whilst someone acts in a manner toward you that infuriates, frustrates, or irritates you. Even things like how humans act, how they speak, how they fragrance, and even how they commonly deliver themselves can "Hook" us.

If we fall for the lure, we're giving the opportunity character authority over how we behave. This may additionally

additionally furthermore then activate an unhelpful reaction.

Whether or no longer we pick out out to get or stay addicted is absolutely as an awful lot as us.

2.   Don't permit them to obtain you.

We regularly allow the mindset of the alternative man or woman to trouble or get worse us. Through our frame language and tone of voice, the alternative character may additionally moreover furthermore see that we're speaking this. This truly makes things greater complex.

Don't fall for the emotive and derogatory feedback that others might also make.

three. Listen, then pay attention yet again.

Make an try and appear and sound attentive even as speakme face-to-face, you have to appear engaged, nod your head, and hold close to eye touch.

When talking over the phone, you need to once in a while say, "Uh Hu - I See."

The possibility of the opposite character being more low cost will growth if they enjoy that you care approximately them and are interested by their hassle.

4. Apply names

One of the coziest topics a person might also pay interest is their name. It implies that you have mentioned them as a completely specific man or woman. It's important to keep away from overdoing it because of the fact the alternative person can perceive it as patronizing.

Make advantageous they may be familiar together with your call and that you will be liable for the problem.

five. DO NOT Accuse

Don't assign blame to every body or something else. It might be very tempting to start looking for for some thing or a person who is responsible for the problems. Avoid blaming a person the least bit costs.

6.   Beware of people's egos

Avoid interfering

Avoid arguing

Don't provide answers right away.

Give them a danger to vent

Avoid announcing, "Calm down."

7.   Consider it from their attitude.

Too regularly, we assume that the "hard" man or woman is being overly dramatic.

What's the large deal? I'll remedy it right right away, we suppose. For the alternative man or woman, it is a big problem, and they want you to apprehend that.

You do now not should trust the character at the way to widely known that they have got an difficulty.

eight. Voice Tone and Body Language

Be very aware of your tone of voice and body language. We often make conditions worse with out even knowledge it.

Our frame language and tone of voice regularly struggle with what we're pronouncing. Even even though we may be apologizing, our tone and body language may be expressing our irritation and annoyance.

People concentrate with their eyes first, as a result the way you say a few factor can be given more weight than what you're saying.

Additionally, it's essential to talk in a pleasing manner even as dealing with a tough circumstance. This does no longer suggest being "nicey-nicey" or acting submissively.

nine. Avoid the ones terms

Particularly in situations which might be emotionally charged, there are a few phrases that would act as triggers and make people more tough. These encompass:

"You need to,"

"But"

I urge you to

"I need to have you ever,"

It is organisation coverage.

You or I every cannot.

Buzz or Jargon words

"Sorry"

"I will strive,"

The Five Steps to Resolution of Conflict

At this element there's no verbal exchange the least bit amongst humans. This segment makes a speciality of people apart from you. It equips you with the vital talents you need to treatment the conflict amongst each events. It is probably co-employees for your enterprise, people of your family or simply any humans you have as friends and care approximately.

Resolution of a dispute or trouble among or greater parties is the definition of conflict choice, however is there a right or incorrect approach to address struggle? What outcomes give up end result from lousy battle decision? Since every employee has a completely particular character, set of dreams, and thing of view, disagreements will commonly upward thrust up at paintings.

Anyone on top of things must expand powerful warfare manipulate abilties as that is the high-quality way to preserve disputes from impeding personnel' career advancement. The 5 steps to resolving a conflict are indexed beneath.

Define the struggle's starting inside the first step.

The more information you have got approximately the issue's root purpose, the much less tough it will likely be at the way to make contributions to its answer. Asking a series of questions, collectively with, "When did you experience disillusioned? ", will help you purchased the information you require. Do you watched this prevalence and that one are associated? "How did this incidence start? "

You, as a manager or supervisor, ought to offer each facets an possibility to give an cause of their aspect of the situation. It will help you realise the situation higher and display that you are objective. Say "I see" or "uh huh" as you are taking notice of every disputant to just accept the records and encourage them to hold speaking to you.

Step is to look past the incident.

The component of view of the problem is often what makes anger make bigger and in the long run culminate in a screaming warfare or distinct apparent and disruptive final results.

The battle also can have originated from a small recollect that passed off months within the past, but the anxiety has reached a problem in which the 2 sports within the period in-between are attacking every first rate individually rather than managing the actual hassle. You can persuade them to appearance past the incident that set them off to discover the real reason inside the tranquility of your workplace. Again, asking insightful questions may be beneficial. For instance, "What do you expect occurred proper here? ", "When do you be given as true with the trouble among you within the beginning advanced?

Step three: Ask for solutions.

The subsequent section is to ask each stakeholder to choose out capability changes to the situation after amassing their views. Ask the events all yet again for their suggestions: "How are we able to enhance our relationship? As a mediator, you want to be a skilled reader of body language and an attentive listener who is privy to each linguistic nuance.

By directing the communique far from accusing each unique and in the direction of functionality answers to the dispute, you can encourage the disputants to region down their guns and begin working collectively.

Step four: Come up with answers that each events can agree on.

Searching for the extraordinary line of movement, you pay attention. Describe the benefits of various principles, no longer simply from every one of a kind viewpoints but additionally in phrases of the benefits to the corporation. For example, you may argue that higher teamwork and collaboration are vital to well deal with departmental and institution worrying situations.

Chapter 11: Dealing With Difficult Coworkers

Find the person who irritates you. You might not be privy to the amount to which a coworker irritates you on a deeper, non-public degree in case you are used to experiencing simplest moderate ache from their bothersome behaviors and quirks on a everyday basis. Consider the coworker you bitch approximately to your friends or family the maximum, the best who reasons interactions to smash your day, or the simplest you may in no way want to percent an elevator with. Spend some time particularly figuring out her or him.

Identify the high-quality purpose this character makes you so indignant. Start with the useful resource of being unique about how you enjoy approximately this individual. Determine the emotions evoked rather than making sweeping generalizations like "She's the maximum obnoxious man or woman within the global." Irritation? Insignificance? Disappointment? You can use this list to locate the right phrases to unique your sentiments. The act of merely identifying your feelings has a chilled cognitive impact that allows you to undertake a trouble-centered perspective. Likewise, pinpoint the precise actions a coworker takes that worsen you. By focusing on what devices you off, you could alternate your response from "I cannot tolerate being round him" to "I expect it's far mainly disrespectful even as she talks over people in meetings."

Recognize that your response to that individual is comments. Become a mirror for the opportunity individual. Consider what you may discover approximately your self from the manner you spoke back to that individual. Think about what this man or woman is modeling for you as an instance of "how no longer to be," as an instance, Does comparing your coworker's continual forgetfulness on your proclivity for structures and enterprise make you recognize that those are features you need to assemble upon in addition, prompting a exchange in career path? It's additionally probably that a coworker's actions will make you want to artwork on any anxieties or insecurities you have were given. If a coworker constantly steals the display, ask yourself if it's miles really worth it given your worry of coming off as conceited if you did the same. Now flip the script: Consider whether or not or not you would love to art work on improving your capability to awareness on your accomplishments in preference to boiling in resentment. Make it your top precedence to achieve this.

Stop Apologizing

The phrase "sorry" is overused and has misplaced its this means that that due to the fact absolutely everyone makes use of it at the same time as some thing is going wrong.

How often do you concentrate

I'm sorry approximately that. Please offer the specifics, and I'll cope with this for you.

If you really ought to mention "sorry," make certain to do it as a trouble of an entire sentence. (Again, it's far wonderful to provide the man or woman's name.) "I'm sorry you have not acquired that records as promised Mr. Smith."

You produce other options except apologizing.

Empathize

This trouble turned into extensively defined in Chapter 2 of this e-book. When interacting with a difficult man or woman, it is important to maintain in mind that:

First, cope with their sentiments before tackling their problem.

It's powerful to deal with a person's feelings via displaying empathy.

Empathy simply calls for elegance of what the opportunity character is announcing and feeling, no longer agreement.

In essence, the message

"I am aware of the manner you revel in."

It is going with out saying that you have to be honest to your reaction; in any other case, the person will experience it and experience patronized.

Examples of how to reveal empathy encompass

"I can see why you are indignant,"

or

"I understand what you suggest"

Once extra, those responses have to be honest.

Create rapport

It may be beneficial to encompass yourself inside the image while responding with empathy every so often.

"I can relate to the manner you enjoy because of the fact I too dislike it at the equal time as that takes location to me."

Building rapport and taking the possibility man or woman's facet are the consequences of doing this.

When utilising this reaction, a few people worry that it'll result in

"Well, then, why do not you're taking movement?"

Most people won't react this manner within the occasion that they apprehend your humanity and feel of motive.

If they do, hold empathizing and provide an reason in your course of movement to the man or woman.

Don't Over-promise and Under-deliver

Don't make a rod for your very very own once more thru saying something in an try and recovery a problem.

In attempting occasions, we are frequently tempted to make tough-to-keep commitments.

We use terms like

I'll solve this this afternoon and contact you lower back.

It is probably difficult to treatment it "this afternoon." Better to simply say

"I'll have things resolved through noon the next day".

They will bear in mind you're wonderful in case you call them once more that day or early the subsequent morning.

Keep in thoughts that your approach won't be continuously a achievement.

There isn't always any thriller components; preserve in thoughts that everybody critiques occasional anger and which you might not always be able to appease anybody.

However, the bulk of humans inside the world are practical human beings, and if you deal with them as such, they will react to you greater favorably.

More Considerations:

These pointers are in large part supposed to help us in managing difficult individuals after a mistake.

Even at the same time as we've now not completed a few component incorrect, we often need to address tough people, but those humans are often hard and won't listen to what we have to mention.

Therefore, we need to workout assertive conduct that allows us to express our desires, goals, and emotions to extraordinary humans in a clean, confident manner with out violating their human rights in any way.

5 annoying terms to avoid using at paintings to avoid sounding passive antagonistic.

People are tired of the jargon used within the place of business, so if the response is "nowadays" or "this week," you are no longer by myself. As films and tweets making fun of overused expressions like "in line with my closing electronic mail" and "circle once more" amass thousands and heaps of likes, you can pay interest the collective, weary sigh of employees across the internet.

Recent Slack research indicates that sixty three% of personnel find out it "off-placing" whilst coworkers talk using company jargon, and 78% stated they chorus from speaking or sending messages to keep away from using it. The test's findings are primarily based on survey data from 2,000 American far flung and hybrid employees amassed in January.

Even nevertheless, 89% of employees admitted to the use of workplace lingo to "sound more expert" or "maintain place of work norms" in conversations with customers, managers, and coworkers.

Let's test the pinnacle 5 place of work jargons to keep away from on the component of advice for reinforcing workplace communique:

1. 'ASAP'

Why it's far worrying: According to Jaime DeLanghe, senior crucial of product manipulate at Slack, "ASAP" is complicated because it "communicates urgency with out definition. Everyone's "ASAP" has a incredible that means; for instance, your boss's "ASAP" can mean the give up of the day, at the same time as yours may additionally moreover endorse the prevent of the week. This can increase war and reason delays at work.

What to mention in location of that: Pick a particular day or hour. For instance, career advertising consultant Emily Liou indicates which includes, "Is it feasible to deliver me this via using EOD?" in a request to someone; this can allow the recipient to reply with a more practical timeline if essential and also you prevent unhappiness on each ends.

2. "Keep me updated."

Why it irritates me: Like "ASAP," this word is ambiguous about what's predicted, regular with DeLanghe. You do now not want to look like a helicopter mom, DeLanghe warns. It can also sound redundant or propose a loss of believe, mainly in a control dating.

What to mention as an possibility: Establish recommendations, such as specific motion phrases or quantifiable measurements, for the way frequently you and the individual with whom you're speakme need to fulfill or communicate the problem. It's an lousy lot extra recommended to apply phrases like "Please update me on X date or at the same time as X milestone has been completed," for instance.

3. A "institution participant"

Why it irritates me: Even on the equal time as meant as a supplement, announcing a person is a "crew player" or asking them to "be a set player" can pop out as commanding, steady with DeLanghe. Workers have handled pretty some strain and unexpected issues, and this kind of remark can sound like it's far encouraging overwork.

What to mention instead: There are many greater uplifting expressions you may use to unique your gratitude for a coworker. It's in truth beneficial expressing gratitude or joy which you are a member of the company.

Chapter 12: Dealing With Difficult Boss At Workplace

Thoughts constantly skip my mind as quickly as I advice people on this specific section of dealing with a difficult boss due to my enjoy at home. As a younger boy my mum can also need to come another time from work continuously searching compelled and worn-out. One day I decided to have a touch conversation collectively together with her and she or he defined to me how her boss come to be usually stressful her on the office. She commonly describe scenarios in which her boss need to publicly insult her ridicule her in the front of various colleagues. I however don't forget the day she came yet again domestic crying because of the truth her boss demoted her for no cause and decreased her profits through almost eighty%. According to James Clear in his e-book on Atomic Habits, Past experience whether or not applicable or terrible on occasion shapes our behavior and behavior. Thoughts of those terrible revel in made me to craft out a few suggestions to make the most of a tough scenario and emerge powerful over a toxic boss.

People often declaration, "My boss needs your resource - they may be a whole psycho, once I supply an purpose behind what I do for a technique.

In reality, it is possibly no longer the case for the reason that there are quality approximately 1 in 100 people who are psychopaths in elegant. It's quite no longer going that your records center's network systems supervisor is a psychopath. However, the consequences on you is probably excessive if you artwork for a person who famous poisonous behavior, together with bullying or hostility.

What are you able to consequently do about it? Here are some pointers to help you cope with a awful boss.

1. . Decide whether to remain or depart.

Making a excessive preference approximately whether or not or not to live or leave is step one in dealing with a poisonous enterprise organization. Consider how significantly the condition is affecting your feelings and highbrow health if you enjoy constrained. If you select out to live, it's miles vital to study some coping abilties to lessen how negatively their conduct could have an effect for your intellectual fitness.

2. Work hard to avoid being a intention.

Avoid becoming a victim or, thru extension, a target if making a decision to live. You could anticipate which means fending off problem and keeping your head down, which might be required, but it could moreover propose the complete opposite. Perform your duties with utmost care. Although it does no longer propose you need to suck up to your company, recollect going as far as you could to make certain their fulfillment. Despite having terrible manage, it will make you a good deal much less of a purpose and those will phrase your professionalism. Trust me, you won't be the extraordinary one to look at this.

Yes, you'll in all likelihood make your manager appearance better inside the eyes of his or her superiors, and perhaps this will result in their getting promoted. However, it may not be a awful component in the event that they get promoted a few region else and a long way from you.

three. Avoid being sucked in.

People who're toxic love to draw you into their drama. Avoid falling for that.

Keep your emotional distance from them truly so it's miles secure. Be courteous, honest, and concise. When you hold a stable emotional distance from a person, you're defensive yourself from their ugly behaviors or moves and persevering with to behavior yourself in a professional and beneficial way at the identical time.

They might also moreover to begin with discover this annoying, but through way of acting "strictly professionally," it offers them little leeway to move and annoy you. Try to consider them as in reality some other a part of your place of job, no worse than the printer this is usually jamming or the awful merchandising machine espresso.

four.   Don't sneer.

Distance your self from the source to hold your sanity intact. This consists of keeping apart and differentiating the damaging individual from yourself.

Even if you do now not apprehend or like them, do no longer belittle them. Speaking nicely of others or as a minimum restraining oneself from doing so is a powerful example of emotional intelligence. If you need to vent, do it a ways from the place of job.

If your coworkers are also struggling, you could assist them thru listening sympathetically, but watch out that any conversations do not flip unpleasant or private. Consider concerning HR if you accept as true with there may be a situation of bullying, intimidation, or harassment. It leads me to my next difficulty.

5. Maintain thorough information.

Keep thorough, real statistics of any fallacious or abusive behavior you come across, and do now not beautify.

You might be requested sooner or later to resource a grievance, both your personal or someone else's. In either situation, your potential to offer specific, in-depth examples out of your very own critiques can extensively improve your argument.

Vague allusions, unsupported anecdotes, rumour, or remarks from 1/three sports don't help a criticism get very a protracted manner. Your case might be bolstered if you can show a sample of volatile conduct thru established proof. You might not possibly enhance very a long manner if you do not preserve thorough and correct information.

Chapter 13: Dealing With Difficult Family Members

Few human beings are spared the hard responsibility of interacting with tough own family participants. Whether you have unkind, unappreciative, untrustworthy, or outright toxic loved ones, using optimistic verbal exchange techniques and battle choice strategies will help you respond to family drama in the appropriate way and get again to taking detail in circle of relatives time.

There are diverse techniques you may behave spherical your member of the family to hold peace, counting on the form of individual you're managing and their particular disturbing situations. To engage in a manner that is least probably to purpose battle, remember what you apprehend about this individual and their everyday inclinations.

Don't waste some time attempting to persuade someone else behavior because you cannot. You do have some effect over your behavior, regardless of the fact that. If you do no longer like what you be conscious in a difficult family member, Debbie Mandel, MA, a stress-discount professional and train, is of the same opinion which you need to cope with the nice component you may manipulate: the way you act and react.

1.   Meet on a impartial vicinity

Having conversations in an environment in that you every experience at ease might sell calm. Consider having the event or hobby take vicinity some different vicinity in case you or a member of your circle of relatives has remarkable difficulties with the contemporary-day website. Meeting for Christmas at a hired occasion location is probably more comfortable than doing it at Mom's house, as an example, because of the fact people have a propensity to act better even as they may be in public.

2. Keep Your Eyes on the Prize

Think of all the property you admire approximately your member of the family earlier than you meet them, and make a mental difference among who they are as someone and their conduct. You'll be higher prepared to address the disturbing behaviors in case you deliver attention to the tremendous in area of the poor. This is because of the fact you won't already be under lots of tension earlier than assembly them, so as to make it simpler in case you need to talk calmly with them.

3. Place Boundaries on Conversations

An "I" announcement furthermore creates a conducive environment for powerful problem-fixing. It's k to quit a tough communication with a tough member of the family because of the fact the extra you speak, the much less powerful the communication may be, and the conflict may also additionally worsen. For example, you can say, "I can not talk with you at the same time as you are yelling due to the truth I am traumatic and uncomfortable," after which ask, "Can we come back to this conversation in any respect yet again at the same time as we're calmer?" Sometimes it's far better to surrender a difficult communique with a difficult family member. Tell the man or woman you may not have a poor communicate with them, and then continuously uphold that barrier.

four. Propose a Break

Allow yourself to leave the conversation for a 2d in case you revel in it is moving into a bad or terrible route. If you experience too crushed with the aid of the conversation and would really like to stop speaking with them, say, "I've loved talking with you. Let's positioned a pin on this talk for now." You also can say, "I'm feeling a bit beaten. Let's communicate this all once more." If you experience the communication is going too a long way, you could say, "I'm going to get a few sparkling air for a few minutes."

5. Request their evaluations on what you said.

Frequently, humans will misinterpret your phrases so that it will argue with you. Ask them something like, "What is your interpretation of what I simply said?" at the identical time as you assume that taking vicinity so you can deal with any misunderstandings proper away.

6. Prepare Your Mind for Conversation

Based on your preceding interactions with this character, picture how this interplay will pass. Family individuals who are difficult to address often display off specific behaviors which may be easy to spot when you become aware about them. Mentally prepare yourself to cope with any situations you assume also can moreover upward push up based definitely totally on their earlier behavior. You would possibly discover that doing this makes it simpler in case you need to reply as it needs to be.

www.ingramcontent.com/pod-product-compliance
Lightning Source LLC
Chambersburg PA
CBHW071442080526
44587CB00014B/1962